# SERVING THE DIFFICULT CUSTOMER

## A How-To-Do-It Manual for Library Staff

## KITTY SMITH

*HOW-TO-DO-IT MANUALS
FOR LIBRARIES*

*Number 39*

NEAL-SCHUMAN PUBLISHERS, INC.
New York, London 1993

Published by Neal-Schuman Publishers, Inc.
100 Varick Street
New York, NY 10013

Printed and bound in the United States of America

**Library of Congress Cataloging-in-Publication Data**

Smith, Kitty, 1945-
    Serving the difficult customer: a how-to-do-it manual for library
staff / Kitty Smith.
        p.    cm. -- (How-to-do-it manuals for libraries  ;  no. 39)
    Includes index.
    ISBN  1-55570-161-2
    1. Libraries and readers--United States. 2. Customer relations.
3. Interpersonal communication--United States.    I. Title.
II. Series.
Z711.S66 1994
025.5--dc20                              93-46452
                              CIP

For Jim, for helping me to see that we are here only to learn;
for Joe, for helping me to learn to see with the heart; and
for Jeanne, for helping me understand gentle strength.

# CONTENTS

# PREFACE

For over 100 years, the library profession has addressed issues related to communicating with, and serving, the needs of our communities and constituents. Profiles of communities have changed—from immigrant to ethnic to socioeconomic groups—reflecting a changing population. Modern management theory has framed the concept of service to include not only patrons or "external customers" but also the constituents within our own organizations, our fellow employees or "internal customers." Within the last few decades euphemisms such as "problem patron" have been created by concerned, but perplexed, library staff to describe the persons or groups that they perceive as the primary source of discomfort or disruption of routine service. The profiles of these "problem people" vary, but the concerns they raise remain constant. Difficult or potentially difficult people continue to present library personnel with communication and behavioral challenges. Too often we have not framed these challenges so that practitioners on the front lines of service can cope with difficult situations, instead of merely complaining about them or responding counterproductively. Staff training often neglects to emphasize the behavioral and informational issues.

All too often, the special groups of people whom we label as "problems" (e.g., the homeless "street person" or the "latchkey" child) are convenient *scapegoats* for our own frustration and inability to deal effectively with the everyday people who habitually or only occasionally exhibit troublesome behavior. All too frequently we thrust the blame for difficult situations squarely on the shoulders of the other person when the underlying problem actually lies in the communication pattern between us and the other party. Instead of changing our role from "victim" to "equal partner" in interactions, thereby taking charge of our own feelings and responses, we often allow ourselves no alternative except a passive, defensive, and ineffective response.

Consequently, this book will address difficult behaviors and situations from a different perspective—one that has us taking *responsibility for our attitudes* and *ownership of our behavior* in interdependent (though problematic) relationships and interactions. Whether we are dealing with a street person, a *normal* patron, a co-worker, a friend, a family member, or *the boss*, we are much more likely to experience an effective and mutually satisfying resolution to the problem by shifting our frame of reference from the problem-patron approach to the difficult-customer approach, from a position of defensiveness and blame to one of assertive understanding and shared problem-solving. The goal is to gain a different perspective, to recognize that our difficult customers may be not only those patrons who represent wider social problems but also our *normal* patrons—the people we live and work with or who work for us. Any of these people may present us with behavior that we find difficult. We ourselves may be someone else's difficult customer!

This book will focus on specific mistaken attitudes and behaviors on the part of *both* parties to the difficulty, rather than on one party or another. While some attention will be paid to selected examples of larger societal problems impinging on library services (i.e., homelessness and the "latchkey" phenomenon), most of this book will address the attitudes, feelings, values, and communication problems experienced and presented by library staff and the majority of the people with which they must interact each day. Its chapters will explore a variety of difficult situations and their probable causes. Further, it will recommend strategies and tactics that staff at all levels can use to empower themselves and better handle difficult and potentially difficult situations and behavior.

The overarching themes of this book are *self-change*, *understanding*, and *commitment*. While specific methods are recommended in these pages to help the reader move in the direction of these goals, true understanding, commitment, and change can take place only in our own minds and hearts. Dealing with difficult interactions requires that we make a conscious commitment to act courageously and assertively. We do not have to remain the passive victims of the difficult customers we encounter every day. By recognizing and understanding the *interactive* aspects of difficult behavior, and the important role we play in these occurrences, we can take positive actions to further our mutual interests (win-win), get along better with others, and function as productively as possible. If we are willing to accept the challenge to *try on* some new understandings and new behaviors, we can empower ourselves to stop scapegoating and start communicating and acting in more effective ways.

# 1 PROBLEM, PROBLEM, WHO'S GOT THE PROBLEM?

Imagine a typical morning at the library. Assorted patrons and staff members are checking books and other materials in and out; asking questions; giving information, directions, and answers; looking things up; quietly browsing; reading; and carrying out myriad other daily tasks. A woman of undetermined age sits alone with two overstuffed shopping bags in the magazine area, effectively keeping other patrons at a distance with a distinct odor emanating from several layers of soiled clothing. A loud male voice suddenly interrupts the daily routine: "What do you mean, it isn't here? I got a card in the mail saying it was being held for me! I drove all the way across town—it took me 30 minutes to get here in this ridiculous traffic. How could you make such a stupid mistake?"

At a meeting later that same day, the director asks the assembled staff for input on the draft of a plan for the library's summer reading program that has just been presented by Barbara, the head of children's services. One of the reference librarians, John, whispers to the others around him, "Why in the world we all have to hear about this kiddie stuff is beyond me. The only one who really cares about it is Barbara. This participatory management business just isn't working. Why waste our time over it?"

By 4 o'clock the library is deluged with the after-school crowd, including two teenagers publicly displaying their affections for each other in a secluded corner, and 14 sixth-graders asking one after another for the same volume of an encyclopedia (which seems to have disappeared) for the identical homework assignment. Amid the turmoil of activity, various staff members have worried about the accuracy of their answers to the 20 newspaper contest questions a telephone patron has called in; listened to complaints from older patrons about the noise level; ejected three boys for horseplay; and tried to get a reticent young woman who asked about treatment options for breast cancer to be more specific about her question.

At 8:45 that evening, as the librarian-in-charge announces that the library will close at nine-o'clock, she again notices the seven-year-old who has been there since three that afternoon, a half-eaten peanut butter sandwich on the table beside him. He says he is waiting for his mother to pick him up. When the librarian dials the boy's home phone number at 9:15, there is no answer.

In order to look at these people and their behavior in new, more productive ways, we first have to give some attention to the words or labels we use to define our problem experiences. Words are powerful symbols. They shape the way we perceive events, think about problems and difficulties, feel about ourselves and other people (as we shall see in subsequent chapters), and respond to those feelings and people.

For example, *the problem patron.* This is a frequent term of choice among library staff when they attempt to capsulize their worst fears or irritations about people they are expected to serve. The word *problem,* when used as an adjective to define a person, lets the speaker accomplish certain objectives, the most obvious of which is to feel in control of the situation. Labeling the other person as a problem allows us to remove ourselves (at least temporarily) from responsibility for the difficult interaction. The other person becomes "the problem" (or at least the perpetrator of it), and we can safely play the role of innocent victim of persecution. This, in turn, allows us to defend ourselves or retaliate against the persecution that the other party now embodies. Any change becomes the responsibility of the other person, not ourselves.

Of course, this is a distorted and overly simplistic view of reality. Labeling a person or a group as a problem provides a convenient way of avoiding personal responsibility. It denies the real nature of social interactions and yields no long-term positive results. Whenever two people interact, they cease to be isolated individuals and become a part of a social system. Systems theory tells us that social systems, like all systems, are made up of not only the various parts but also the interrelationship of those parts. When two people interact, the social system consists of the two individuals *and* their interaction. In the case of problem communications, whatever the underlying source of the difficulty, once the interaction begins, successful communication becomes the responsibility of *both* parties.

Because the problems we experience with other people are so intertwined with our patterns and styles of interaction and communication, the term *problem patron* can be seen as misguided and virtually useless. And our interactions in the library are not limited to patrons alone. Most people who work in libraries and other service organizations interact with other staff members and administrators, as well as colleagues in other organizations. These people, and our interactions with them, powerfully influence the ways we relate to our clients. In a sense, they constitute the culture of our organizations, and the policies, climate, and culture of the organization and our *interactions with other members of the organization* have the greatest effect on how successfully we can interact with our patrons, not the reverse. Therefore, to hold patrons, especially those patrons with the least power and resources, responsible for our frustrations and difficulties in providing service does a disservice to both our patrons and ourselves.

We run into difficult situations with people everyday, *not just with patrons*. Whether it is the ambivalent or indecisive director, the belligerent boss, the silent or passive-aggressive co-worker, or the overly acquiescent employee, interactions with people with behavioral idiosyncrasies can be stressful to a degree far out of proportion to their frequency. Such interactions can be disheartening and discouraging. In the worst instances, they can lead to staff absenteeism, poor productivity, and alienation among staffers and patrons. The term *difficult customer,* therefore, is not limited to the so-called problem patron. Rather, the difficult customer might be anyone with whom we must interact and communicate, either verbally or non-verbally, and with whom communication is so difficult that neither of us can get our needs or goals met. Whether we know the individual personally, whether we have encountered this person repeatedly or have just met him or her for the first time, whether we recognize the person as an external customer, someone who is served by the library, or an internal customer, someone we work with or for in the library, communication and service can be *difficult* to the extent that we seem to be working at cross-purposes toward mutually exclusive goals. We each behave in ways that are viewed by the other as roadblocks to progress rather than as aids.

This state of affairs can be devastating to the very mission and objectives of the library profession, whose essence is the provision of services to people. Difficult behaviors on the part of others often seem contagious. We may start out consciously determined to deal with these difficult people by reasoning with them. However, our well-meant, *normal* methods of communications often fail to persuade these others to *be reasonable.* Indeed, their frustrating, difficult behavior may actually intensify.

In response, out of frustration, we may either flee the situation or slip into a dysfunctional behavior pattern similar to, or at least in sync with, that of our "oppressor," be it an angry retort, a sarcastic remark, a cool pout, or some other form of competitive interaction. Whatever we do, the underlying problem or cause of the difficult behavior does not get resolved. Even worse, it may silently grow until there is little motivation or hope for a rational adult solution. And so the cycle of difficulty keeps turning, often in a downward spiral.

The purpose of this discussion is not to paint a gloomy, even hopeless, picture of communication patterns in libraries, but instead to emphasize a major premise of this book: We tend to treat our patrons—the people we are in business to serve—the way we are treated by our organization and its members and the way we treat ourselves. We may sometimes blame our patrons or our colleagues when the source of our problems really lies somewhere within ourselves or within our organizations. Our power to change things in the organization may be limited, but personal change and empowerment are always well within the realm of possibility. To turn the possibility of change into reality, however, we must be willing to shift our frame of reference; that is, the way we look at, and assess, difficult behavior and the people who manifest it. By raising our awareness and understanding of the operative variables in our communication with difficult customers, whatever their relationship to us, we can start moving out of the pointless blame-and-conflict mode. By learning and practicing basic skills of communication, assertiveness, cooperation, and decision-making, we can begin to seek a common ground of communication and partnership with our clients and our co-workers. This is the true meaning of personal empowerment.

# FROM CONFLICT TO COMMON GROUND

It has been said that whenever two or more people are repeatedly in each others' presence and interacting with each other, over time, there is bound to be conflict sooner or later. This inevitability of conflict holds the possibility of both good and bad outcomes. Conflict can be good for a relationship if differences can be resolved with some degree of satisfaction for both parties (the "win-win" outcome). Along with a satisfactory resolution, the relationship may become stronger and more mutual in nature. However, if "win-lose" is the only perceived option for each party in the dispute or difficulty, the relationship usually suffers, even disintegrates, regardless of who wins. The winner may take the battle, but in the long run he or she is worse off for the damage to the relationship, due to the other party's loss of self-esteem. The "loser" may withdraw, regroup for another direct assault on the enemy, or (because we live under certain social and workplace constraints) go underground, resorting to more indirect and devious ways of achieving his or her goals.

Everyone is someone's difficult person sometime. To repeat: *Everyone* is someone's difficult person sometime. No one is above behaving in a difficult manner when it seems natural. Depending on how much we feel we are in control in certain interpersonal situations, we may become acquiescent, hostile, ambivalent, or withdrawn. For better or worse, every human being who comes to the library is fully equipped with beliefs, values, and feelings that guide her or him in responding to the daily circumstances, decisions, and experiences of life.

It should come as no surprise, especially in a profession requiring a great deal of interpersonal contact, that each person has a social-emotional agenda to work through each day, besides his or her physical and intellectual agendas or "to-do lists." The items on this social-emotional agenda consist of interpersonal interactions or communications that can be characterized by both their *content* and their *process*.

## CONTENT AND PROCESS

Content consists of the thoughts and ideas expressed and exchanged by the person in interactions. Process refers to the feelings, or emotional context, underlying the interactions. Whether positive, negative, or mixed, these feelings, and our ability to be aware of them, are basic to human nature. They are always present to some degree when two or more persons interact. They may be expressed verbally or nonverbally, appropriately or inappropriately. They may be acknowledged and validated by the individual, who may then choose not to directly express them. When an individual unconsciously represses or denies these ideas, the individual may default either to indirect expression or to no expression at all, often with unhealthy results for both parties to the communication.

In relative contrast with task-oriented agendas, the social-emotional agenda can persist over time. While some physical and intellectual tasks can be assigned low priority, or even become unnecessary after a while, one's social-emotional agenda does not simply go away in time. Instead, it is inescapable. Each individual deals with it according to his or her level of skill and awareness.

As with the mental and physical agendas, the individual may be aware, semi-aware, or for all practical purposes unaware of the social-emotional agenda. In terms of communication skills, the person may be exceptionally competent and confident or relatively unequipped to cope with whatever is on his or her own agenda or the other person's agenda. For most people, some contexts and people are easier to cope with than others, and there is a wide variation in the individual skills, confidence, perceptions, and awareness in any given incident or interaction.

Successful communication results in mutual understanding, a sense that the parties are on common ground, with some degree of satisfaction and achievement of objectives on both sides. Unsuccessful communication results in misunderstanding, dissatisfaction, and a win-lose outcome. If there are difficulties within the communication process itself, it does not matter whether problem behavior is occurring on one or both sides. The underlying problem will not be addressed until the communication difficulty has been resolved.

## COMMUNICATING

Perhaps the greatest obstacle to solving problems related to communicating with patrons and providing them with library services is our way of thinking about problems in the first place. It is almost a truism that, in every social system of every type, from the family to the library organization, events occur that may evoke emotional responses, and these situations may lead to further emotional responses to the original emotional response, and so on and so on in an ever ascending (or descending) spiral, without the initial problem ever being acknowledged.

If we shift our thinking from the library context to an example from everyday life, this process might be grasped more easily. Consider the following dialogue:

Spouse A: What in the world happened to you? It's seven thirty! We were due at Mother and Dad's a half hour ago! You could have at least called and let me know you were going to be late!

Spouse B: Give me a break! The car decided to die on me halfway home and I was nowhere near an exit. I couldn't call from the middle of the interstate! When I finally got it started again, I got here as fast as I could. Besides, your parents won't mind if we're a little late.

Spouse A: Well I mind! It seems like we're always late going to see them. Don't you care about their feelings? After all, they keep offering to help us out with the down payment on the new car. I think you should show a little more respect and appreciation.

Spouse B: I *do* appreciate their offer to help! I love that old car, but lately every time I go to work I wonder if I'm going to make it home at all. You know, when it died on me, it was pure luck that I could coast from the passing lane to the shoulder without getting creamed by somebody. I'm pretty shaken up by what happened today. Could we just call your parents and explain? I sure could use some time to relax and clean up before we go.

Spouse A: You need time to relax? What about me? This is the third time in a month I'll have to make excuses for you to my parents. And I was really looking forward to this evening. By the time we get there the evening will be practically shot! And all because of you and that antique you're so sentimental about!

And so it goes—a little ventilating, a little (very little) listening, a little blaming.

There are a number of ways this little scenario could turn out, depending largely on how the individuals choose to see the problem. One possibility is for A, who is feeling discounted, to continue to accuse B of being:

1. overly sentimental about B's old car,
2. irresponsible in the matter of calling when one is going to be late, and
3. uncaring and ungrateful to A's parents (and, by affiliation, to A), and so forth.

Another is for B, who is already under stress from frustration with the car, from the narrow escape from danger on the highway, and from hunger, to:

1. angrily hurl a few accusations back to A about A's lack of understanding and selfishness,
2. stalk out of the room and refuse to go out at all, or
3. withdraw affection and further communication from A for the rest of the evening, and the like.

These are the sorts of options open to people when the problem is oversimplified and is viewed as existing outside of oneself, rather than as something that is more complex (because more than one person is involved), and that is a product of one's personal interpretation of the facts.

Stephen Covey, in his best-selling book on personal change, *The Seven Habits of Highly Effective People*[1], suggests that, quite often, the way we *view* a problem actually *is* the problem. That is, where and with whom we place the blame for our difficulties, and where and with whom we place responsibility for their removal, determine to a large extent the direction of our thoughts, our feelings, and our behavior in a difficult situation.

Many of us take the path of least resistance (i.e., our parental and societal conditioning), concluding that our discomfort, negative feelings, and status as victims are caused by forces and people outside of ourselves. In other words, if only *they* (people, events, facts) were different, then *we* would feel better or behave differently. In reality, however, as Covey explains, we are often unconscious of the fact that we have other options, and that we can and do *choose* to exercise our options in other ways. *Cultural scripting* is very powerful regarding our customary ways of defining and handling problems. However, our customary ways are really no more than deeply ingrained habits, and habits *can* be changed.

Our ability to choose and to change habits is largely related to our evolution as human beings. We are unique among animals, particularly in our brain development, particularly that of the cerebral cortex. Unlike other animals who perceive the world, react, and adapt, we can think about our perceptions and plan our responses *before and after our perceptions occur*. Because of our exceptional brains, we have the ability to learn, to compare new information with previous learning, and to integrate the conclusion into a meaningful body of knowledge for ourselves. We are endowed with the ability to be aware of ourselves as thinking, choosing beings, to remember, to imagine, to assign value, and to choose a course of action in accordance with our values. Indeed, through conscious choice and mental visualization, we can recreate whole scenes without any of the essential elements actually being present, or mentally run through the melody of a favorite song without a physical sound being made or heard. We do this in our minds, or as the saying goes, "in our heads."

It stands to reason that if we have the ability to consider facts and events outside of ourselves, and interpret them in terms of our knowledge and values, we are more than simply slaves to the stimulus-response paradigm, demonstrated so admirably by laboratory rats. Because we can anticipate and review, imagine and mentally rehearse, integrate new learning with our values, and draw conclusions based on many experiences, we are able to choose among many possible responses to many situations, both pleasant and troublesome. Habits develop from repeating a particular response to similar stimuli until the response becomes unconscious and automatic. Conscious recognition that we can choose our responses from among the many more productive and desirable ones available to us, is the first step toward choosing new behaviors and building new habits. The process is similar to that of a pilot programming the chosen course into a plane's automatic pilot.

In light of this different model of thinking and responding to events in our lives, it becomes clear that *we do not have to see ourselves as victims* of hostile, uncomfortable, or otherwise difficult people or environments that supposedly cause our unhappiness, or whom we can conveniently blame. *We have the power to choose* to understand the people in our environment, to explore alternative ways of dealing with difficult people and situations, to risk experimentation with new interpretations and responses, and to draw conclusions that are different from the ones that we have been conditioned to reach and that guide our habitual, and perhaps dissatisfying, responses.

This power to choose change, however, must be exercised consciously from *within* each of us, not imposed or cajoled by someone outside ourselves, if any meaningful change is to be more than temporary. A change in one's behavior (even self-destructive behavior) primarily to please or placate another person is sometimes expedient, but it seldom lasts and is often resented, once the immediate pressure is off. Under such conditions, the new behavior rarely becomes a habit, even if the individual prefers the consequences of the new behavior to the consequences attached to the old.

For example, a smoker could rationalize:

> I won't smoke in my grandmother's presence because she has repeatedly informed everyone in the family that she doesn't approve of it, and that it is hard for her to breathe when she's around cigarette smoke. She nags me constantly about it, but I know she really cares about me and my health. And she's absolutely right. I should quit. Smoking is dreadful for my health. My chances of having a heart attack or lung disease would drop considerably if I quit. I know I promised her I would quit, but this week's schedule at work has been horrendous. I have enough pressure without the added stress of trying to quit smoking. I can't even think about quitting until Friday afternoon, or over the weekend, after things have had a chance to calm down. It's just too hard right now. Just thinking about everything I have to do makes me uptight. Looks like I'm just going to have to live with my guilt about smoking a little longer. [Searching in pockets for cigarette

pack] In the meantime, Granny doesn't have to know about this one. Just one right now isn't going to kill me, and I need it to calm down a little.

What is going on here? On some level the smoker obviously knows the health hazards of smoking, both to himself and to a beloved family member. He also feels guilty about not keeping his promise to his grandmother and shame at incurring her disapproval. But he does not truly *own* his personal responsibility for the current status of his smoking habit. Nor does he admit to himself that it is within his power to choose when he will stop. He acknowledges the possible health consequences, but these are long-term cumulative effects that exist somewhere in the future, not now. At the present moment, since they are not being experienced, they are not being directly related to his current smoking behavior. And his motivation to please his grandmother is conveniently outweighed by his ability to evade her displeasure for the time being.

In other words, he cannot solve his problem habit because he sees it as something *external to himself.* He assigns power over smoking to his grandmother's attitude, to his pressured work schedule, to consequences that may or may not happen years from now, to just about anything available in his environment *except himself.* As long as he can rationalize and minimize the short-term consequences, both physical and interpersonal, he will continue to evade his personal responsibility for quitting and, therefore, will continue to smoke, regardless of occasional twinges of guilt, shame, and shortness of breath.

Just as you cannot give something to another (including yourself) unless and until you actually possess it, you cannot permanently change an unproductive or destructive habit (e.g., your typical role or pattern of behavior in interpersonal communications) unless and until you acknowledge ownership of it and exercise your power and ability to initiate change from within.

Like a door that can only be opened from the inside, commitment to permanent personal change and improved relationships with others cannot be bought, forced, or manipulated by others. There is no "quick fix," no single technique or set of tricks that another can use to change us in any permanent sense. Each of us must volunteer to open the door ourselves, by consciously acknowledging our power and by proactively learning and applying new behaviors consistent with a new way of looking at interpersonal problems from the inside out. We don't have to keep doing what we are doing, but we alone have the power to stop one set of behaviors and start doing something else.

# WHO IS A DIFFICULT CUSTOMER?

Everyone can be hard to get along with at certain times, with certain people, under certain circumstances. Everyone loses their temper on occasion or withdraws, and would probably admit to caving in to another person's wants or needs sometimes to avoid a confrontation. However, occasional incidents of aggressiveness, nonassertiveness, and other difficult behaviors are not sufficient to permanently label a person as habitually "difficult."

Sometimes the conditions you work or live under can bring out the worst in everyone. The *corporate culture* can be a powerful force in determining people's behavior on the job. Although the mission of most libraries is to provide services to and through people, libraries, as institutions, are not exempt from the tendency of all large or growing organizations to become bureaucratic, rule-bound, and authoritarian, especially if they exist within a parent organization (e.g., a corporation, a local government or school system, or an academic setting) that is itself impersonal and bureaucratic. When the pressures of such a climate build, everyone can become defensive and irritable. When the pressures become too great, people may psychologically or physically withdraw.

When resources are perceived as scarce, people tend to become competitive. And when internal competition is the rewarded norm, practically every interaction with someone outside of one's team can become a win-lose battle. Anyone can think of individuals who could be described by family and friends as sweet and gentle and by co-workers and employees as ruthless and insufferable (and vice versa). Therefore, it is crucial to begin by distinguishing between the person and the behavior, and to determine the effect of the organizational climate on the individual, and whether you have any power to effect change in that organizational culture and climate. The last may or may not be possible, given your position or status in the organization. However, you always have the power to try to deal with another individual's difficult behavior without permanently dismissing the individual as a problem.

The organizational climate is not the only outside force that can influence one's behavior. Sometimes *personal circumstances* can produce a sudden behavioral change (e.g., illness, death of a loved one, change in a relationship, money problems, and fear of unemployment). A person's response to these difficulties depends on how much physical, mental, and emotional strength they bring to the situation, and how they have learned to deal with such difficulties in the past. Responses can vary from cheerful denial to intense irritability, from having "the blues" to hyperactive, out-of-control behavior. Whatever the reason for it, you will almost certainly notice when someone's mood or behavior is out of character for them.

This out-of-character behavior is the key to distinguishing someone who is experiencing normal ups and downs of life, from someone who is truly and habitually a difficult person. Normally friendly and cooperative people do not regularly behave in ways that prohibit others from getting along with them or working with them. Over time and through regular interaction with most people, you learn how to tell when they are having an occasional bad day or they are in an especially good mood. Dealing with their normal ups and downs is not a burden to anyone, and they tend to reciprocate by being sensitive to your ups and downs when they occur. People who know each other well, and who have established good working relationships with one another, tend to treat each other with empathy and give each other the benefit of the doubt.

The truly difficult customer, on the other hand, is the one who seems totally unwieldy. His or her behavior consistently disrupts or interferes with your getting things done as you would like or within your time frames. These individuals seem to make it impossible for you to get along with them or get cooperation from them.

At this point in the discussion, it is important to keep in mind that it is your *own* perceptions that determine the degree of difficulty. Some people may be difficult only to you. Others may be difficult for everyone around them. The point is that, with rare exception, the problem lies in the *interaction*—the *relationship*—rather than in the individuals themselves. How you and the other person perceive each other, and the extent to which each of you is able to tolerate and deal with the other's conduct, determines how big a problem you have.

In the case of the normal people described above, you have probably learned to perceive them in a generally positive (or at least neutral) light, despite their ups and downs, for which you have developed an acceptable degree of tolerance. These people may appear to be like you in many ways. In fact, you may assume that they share many of the values and goals that you hold dear, even when they do not.

With *your* truly difficult people, on the other hand, your experience may have resulted in a general negative perception of them, despite their good moments, and your tolerance threshold has become quite low. They seem different from you in many ways, and these perceived differences only add to the impression that they are impossible to get along with or to control. (They, by the same token, may see *you* as difficult or impossible!) Responses that seem to work with other people don't seem to work with these folk, a fact that further reinforces your negative perceptions of them.

People tend to describe other's personalities with labels that match their perceptions of them and their behavior. For example, you may describe a friend as steadfast or firm, and call a difficult person stubborn or rigid, when both are exhibiting essentially the *same behavior*. Remember, it is *your* perceptions that determine who is *your* difficult person. The difficulty results when two people try to fulfill their own desires or get their own needs met through dissimilar means, when they hold divergent opinions, when they are acting from different motivations or attitudes, or when they cherish different values or goals. Each wants a different outcome from the interaction. Each sees the other as unyielding or interfering, disinclined to negotiate or capitulate.

It should be obvious at this point that when people behave toward you in difficult ways, you may have a tendency to take it more personally than intended. If the person exhibiting the difficult behavior is an occasional visitor or nontraditional patron or other relative stranger, you might react (or overreact) as if a relationship existed between you and the behavior was specifically and intentionally targeted at *you* when it is not. In reality, when dealing with relative strangers, you can't always tell whether their difficult behavior is symptomatic of a habitual style of communication or whether they are simply having a bad day. Nevertheless, you may react in negative and unproductive ways, instead of choosing to respond assertively and productively.

# FROM CHAOS TO CONTROL

Because it is our perceptions of a situation or a relationship that determine for us the degree of difficulty, we need to pay close attention to our perceptions, especially when planning strategies for dealing with difficult people. Our perceptions are based on our observations of another person's behavior, colored by our own personal goals, values, attitudes, and beliefs. Therefore, it makes sense that solutions might begin with our definitions of other people in terms of their *behaviors*, rather than in terms of their *personalities* or *characters*. No one, ourselves included, really has much control over the basic personality traits that have developed from infancy.

But we all do have opportunities in the present to take control of what we say or do next. Regardless of the difficulties we may encounter, we can freely choose to stop doing something we have habitually done, and start doing something we have not typically done. In other words, we can change our own behaviors and, thereby, influence another person to change behavior, without concerning ourselves with changing other people's personalities or lamenting the frequently unproductive habitual patterns of behavior we and others have exhibited in the past.

The next chapter offers a more detailed rationale for understanding and categorizing productive and unproductive patterns of interpersonal behavior.

# References

1.  Stephen R. Covey, *The Seven Habits of Highly Effective People: Restoring the Character Ethic*. (New York: Simon and Schuster, 1990), 40.

# 2 UNDERSTANDING DIFFICULT BEHAVIOR

Some difficult behaviors are relatively easy to cope with and change. Others are more troublesome, require exceptional concentration and effort, and are less tractable to change. Various methods exist for categorizing behaviors, and some of these will be explored in this chapter, along with steps for dealing with them more effectively.

## TYPES OF DIFFICULT CUSTOMERS

First, consider some basics regarding human relationships and communication:

1. Working relationships, whether personal or professional, depend upon communication for survival and growth.
2. Communication consists of both content (the message) and process (the context of the message, usually emotional to a greater or lesser extent).
3. Relationships and communication both depend on the interaction of at least two individuals.
4. Persons at any given point in life are unique products of their inherited physical characteristics; the knowledge, skills, values, beliefs, attitudes, and patterns of behavior they have learned through experience, from family, and from society (what we might call their culture); and their current intentions, desires, and goals.

The emphasis here is on the individual and his or her uniqueness as both a positive value and a potential source of difficulty. We each bring with us tremendous abilities both to create and to destroy in the course of acquiring what we need and desire in life. We seek relationships with others both for mutual help in reaching our individual goals and for the joy inherent in relationships themselves. Although these points may appear obvious in theory, they are often lost in the context of difficult communications, a fact that serves to illustrate the central theme of this chapter: how we differ and how we are the same.

One useful way of analyzing interpersonal behavior is to look at interactions in terms of two dimensions:

1. an individual's locus of control, and
2. his or her level of response.

Let us look first at the issue of control. When observing our own or another person's behavior, it is helpful to ask ourselves the following questions:

- Does the person seem to be in an active or passive mode?
- Does he or she seem to have a sense of personal power and control, or does this person appear to be at the mercy of outside forces and other people?
- Does behavior seem to come from within—that is, to be self-motivated by a desire to be in charge of one's feelings and actions, to accomplish a task, or to reach a goal?
- Or does it seem reactive—that is, to be driven by a need to protect or defend oneself from the real or perceived power of others?

What about the level of responsiveness? Does the individual seem sensitive to and aware of the other person's feelings, interests, and needs, while communicating his or her own? Or is he or she dictatorial, manipulative, and noncommunicative?

Using these two aspects of behavior and communication as dimensions for analysis, we might categorize human interactions into four types as illustrated in the accompanying diagram (see Fig. 2-1).

Differences among these behavior patterns can be distinguished by:

1. the relative degree of personal power and control the person typically exercises in interactions, and
2. the degree to which the person is able to consider and respond to the needs of others with whom he or she interacts.

Any one of these might typify the behavior of our own difficult customers, because of either its inherent nature or its relative appropriateness in a specific set of circumstances.

At this point it is important to remember that the accompanying model, while useful in understanding and finding our way around the sometimes confusing topography of interpersonal communication, *is* only a model. Although this model is commonly encountered in the literature about personality and behavior, it basically deals only with two dimensions of communication behavior. No

FIGURE 2-1   Types of Interactive Behavior

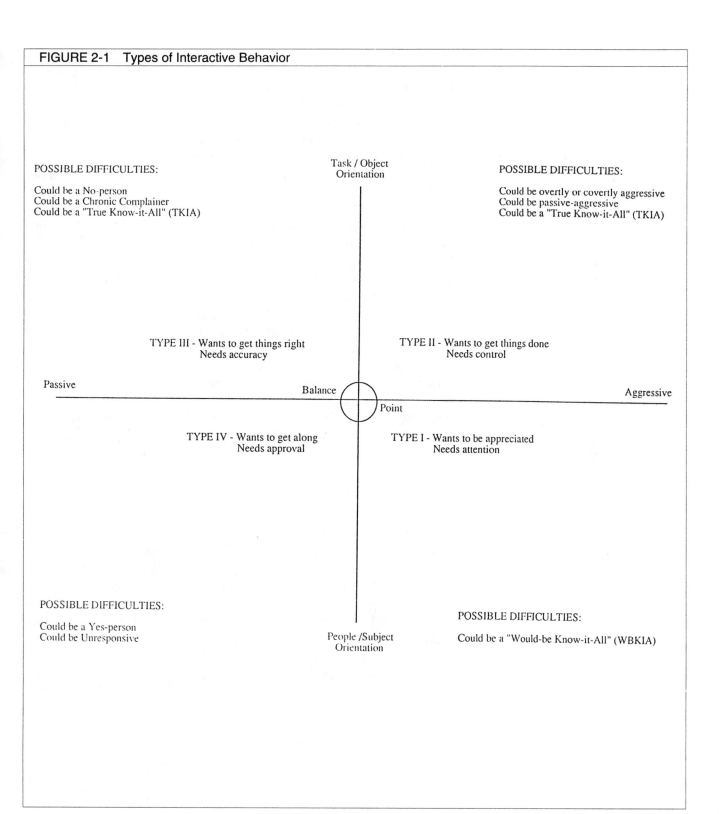

POSSIBLE DIFFICULTIES:

Could be a No-person
Could be a Chronic Complainer
Could be a "True Know-it-All" (TKIA)

POSSIBLE DIFFICULTIES:

Could be overtly or covertly aggressive
Could be passive-aggressive
Could be a "True Know-it-All" (TKIA)

Task / Object
Orientation

TYPE III - Wants to get things right
Needs accuracy

TYPE II - Wants to get things done
Needs control

Passive

Balance

Aggressive

Point

TYPE IV - Wants to get along
Needs approval

TYPE I - Wants to be appreciated
Needs attention

POSSIBLE DIFFICULTIES:

Could be a Yes-person
Could be Unresponsive

People /Subject
Orientation

POSSIBLE DIFFICULTIES:

Could be a "Would-be Know-it-All" (WBKIA)

model of human interactions, no matter how detailed or sophisticated, can fully capture all the nuances of an individual interaction between two unique individuals at a particular place and time. We are using this particular model simply as a tool to understand some patterns of difficult human behavior, one of which may be typical of a given individual. However, we must remember that there are circumstances unique to every interaction that might evoke one of the other patterns of behavior. We all do things that may seem out of character for us from time to time. We all experience mood changes to some extent or have a bad day now and then. Just as a map is not the territory, what a person will say and do in a specific context cannot always be predicted, even when we can identify his or her usual mode of behavior. Behavior may provide clues to the individual's character or personality but a person is always more than his or her typical behavior, or feelings, or values, taken by themselves, can ever define. Only by actively listening and observing another person's verbal and nonverbal behavior during a specific interaction can we begin to understand what is really going on and determine what our appropriate response should be.

Because the model we are using here is only two-dimensional, these four behavior types may seem overly simplified and generalized, like the horoscope column in the daily newspaper. Nevertheless, the following descriptions should provide some insight into the behavior pattern categories defined by the illustration and serve as the basis for understanding the types of difficult behavior explored later in this book.

## TYPE I BEHAVIOR

*Type I* depicts characteristic behaviors of people we might call self-determined or self-actualizing. They are likely to feel comfortable as leaders and as team members or working alone, if the situation requires. They see problems as challenges rather than as burdens, and they are realistic about their own limitations. They make mistakes and learn from them. They seek help from others who have the resources they lack, without envy or self-effacement. They actively plan and prioritize, setting and striving for reasonable goals, and they help others do the same. They behave assertively, while respecting others' ideas, listening to them, and recognizing their feelings.

They are independent yet caring. They lead by mutual respect and encouragement of others' participation in decision making, rather than by demanding obedience to their authority. They inspire creativity and assertiveness in others, rather than feel threatened by it. They get satisfaction from a job well done, and they give credit where it is due. They gather information and share facts with everyone, not gossip and rumors. They communicate with openness and honesty and inspire the same in others. They empower themselves and others with the confidence and competence needed to solve problems and conflicts. Type I people provide opportunities for others to act in their own interests and to grow.

Type I behavior is not difficult for other people in and of itself. Of the four types, Type I is most likely to promote and enhance strong, productive relationships between individuals. This does not mean, however, that Type I individuals never get into trouble with other people.

Ideally their behavior should enable them to function independently, behave assertively, exert personal power, and fulfill individual needs through personal responsibility and initiative. But the reality is that individual needs and goals differ from person to person. The interests of one person may differ from those of another, or of the group as a whole, and one's behavior may interfere with another person achieving his or her objectives.

Rather than mutual cooperation, Type I behavior may set the stage for resistance or conflict. When this happens, the Type I person might withdraw when confrontation would be more effective. In an effort to empower people to satisfy their own needs, the Type I leader may sometimes inadvertently let things get out of control by failing to exert authority and control appropriately. In an ideal world, mutual respect is the basis of power, and differences are celebrated. In the real world, people are often perfectionists, intolerant, and resistant of others whom they see as different from themselves. People do not always treat each other with respect.

## TYPE II BEHAVIOR

People who exhibit *Type II* behavior are similar to Type I people, especially in their task-orientation and their desire to operate independently and to feel a measure of autonomy and control over their environments. Where Type IIs differ is in their tendency to behave aggressively, rather than assertively, and in their responses to the needs and feelings of others. Type IIs do not merely wish to be in control of themselves—they seem to want to control others as well. This is particularly true when they feel threatened by people or by circumstances that they perceive as obstacles in their path. The frustration they feel can be expressed in a number of ways, including sometimes arguing and dominating conversations to the extent that the communication seems one-way.

Type IIs want to get things done and often willingly take on tasks and challenges that would terrify less aggressive people. They may appear authoritarian, overbearing, pompous, and selfish, constantly seeking attention and demanding recognition for what they accomplish. They can be especially frustrating to deal with (particularly for Type Is) because they may appear not to care about others' rights to express personal power. If other people try to assert themselves, Type IIs may become even more intrusive and aggressive, to the point of acting hostile and engaging in a power contest.

## TYPE III BEHAVIOR

*Type III* people lean toward the opposite end of the locus of control dimension from Is and IIs. They perceive themselves as relatively less powerful than these two types, and therefore they may constantly seek attention and avoid rejection from them by giving in rather than standing up for themselves. They can be especially intimidated by Type IIs, their diametric opposites, whom they cajole and give in to. Rather than take risks and rise to challenges, they are more likely to seek protection in the acceptance and appreciation of others. They are highly people-oriented and social in their interactions with others. They want to be recognized for their caring, helpful attitudes and behaviors. Maintaining friendly relationships with others is extremely important to them, so much so that they run the risk of alienating and frustrating their more task-oriented associates with their constant chatter about inconsequential matters. While they would probably deny the desire to control others, their excessive efforts to assure themselves of others' goodwill can feel manipulative and controlling to others.

## TYPE IV BEHAVIOR

*Type IV* behavior is characteristic of people who perceive themselves as lacking both personal power and the ability to relate to others. The exact opposite of Type I, Type IVs may behave in very self-protective, rigid ways. They seem to be most comfortable performing tasks that are highly routine or that do not require them to make decisions or exceptions to established rules and procedures. They would rather be left alone than bothered by others who are more people-oriented. If their safety and security are threatened by one of the other types, they retreat into silence. This can be especially frustrating to Type Is and Type IIs who need them to provide information or make a decision. While Type IIIs often communicate too much, Type IVs may communicate too little or not at all. The excessive fawning and talkativeness of Type IIIs can drive Type IVs to internal turmoil and actual physical withdrawal.

Bear in mind that any *extreme* examples of these difficult behavior patterns could be symptomatic of more severe mental or emotional disturbance, especially if accompanied by severe mood swings. If a person's behavior is consistently inappropriate, irrational, and compulsive, there is probably little we or the individual in question can do alone to change it or even cope with it. The most appropriate response in cases like this is to ensure one's own safety and that of others, if there is a threat of physical danger, or to seek the help of people who possess the training and expertise necessary to handle the situation. Depending on the specific circumstances, a library staff member may have to call on police or other emergency personnel for assistance. The scope of this book does not permit the exploration of the most extreme difficult behaviors that might call for institutionalization or psychiatric treatment.[1] However, policies and procedures for handling highly disturbing or dangerous situations in the library would be quite suitable as topics for discussion in a staff development or training program, with experts on hand for consultation.

Of the four types of interpersonal behavior described here, three (Types II, III, and IV) encompass most of the difficult behaviors one is likely to encounter with patrons and/or library staff. Although an individual's dominant mode of behavior might fall neatly into one of the four categories, we all have the capacity to engage in all of the other types of behavior depending on the circumstances and how we perceive ourselves in relation to another person's personal power and sensitivity to us.

# BEHAVIOR AND NEEDS

There is a definite connection between behavior and needs. By watching what people do and say, you may be able to deduce the needs that underlie their behavior. For example, the person who needs attention or appreciation may actively try to take "center stage" and get others to take notice by behaving assertively or aggressively. The shy, silent, or withdrawn person may be feeling a need for safety or security, and so he or she will behave in such a way as to avoid being in the spotlight. However, while some people are skilled observers of human behavior, you should take care not to base your conclusions about another person's motivations simply on what *you* would think, say, or do under similar conditions. Whatever your conclusions, they are the result of taking in sensory data and comparing them with your own values, beliefs, attitudes, and what you have learned from your own experience to be true for you. Your impressions are reality for you, but not reality for everyone everywhere. More specifically, your impressions and conclusions may miss the mark completely in terms of the value, beliefs, attitudes, and intentions of the person whose behavior you are observing. This is not to say that your impressions and conclusions are never accurate or trustworthy. It is just that you cannot be sure without some sort of verification of the data (e.g., giving and getting feedback from the other person and challenging our own biases).

Also, you cannot assume that your understanding of another's (or your own) needs, intentions, and behavior, will automatically enable you to *change* those behavior patterns. For one thing, it is unrealistic to expect that you can change anyone's behavior other than your own. For another, people do not give up habitual behavioral patterns simply because someone else would prefer that they change them. Demands and coercion may produce temporary results but they do not make for permanent change.

If you want your interactions with others, especially with difficult customers, to change, it is far more realistic to begin by understanding your own needs, intentions, and typical behavior patterns, and how they might be a factor in actually maintaining the behaviors of others who are troublesome for you. One effective way to do this is to list examples of the things others say and do that cause you the most difficulty (that is, push your emotional buttons), plus a list of their behaviors that are perfectly acceptable. Then, looking at the list of difficult behaviors, ask yourself: How do I typically respond in these positive interactions with these persons? What about the difficult interactions? Is my behavior more like Type I, Type II, Type III or Type IV in these situations? Am I creating obstacles to reaching an understanding with these persons through my behavior toward them? Where might a change in my behavior with these persons make a positive difference in our ability to communicate successfully?

The brief self-assessment quiz, which may be found in Appendix A, can be used by library staff members alone or in group training to help determine their typical responses to different types of difficult situations.

# CHANGE BEGINS AT HOME

Remember, identifying the problem with the other person—that is, holding the other person responsible for it—does nothing to solve it. Each person in a relationship—whether it is a brief one-time interaction or a long-term association—can be responsible only for his or her own feelings and responses. Eleanor Roosevelt once wisely remarked to the effect that no one can make you a victim without your permission. Whether the outcome of an interaction is positive or negative, both persons have played a role in its success or failure. To deal with others' difficult behavior requires that you take assertive action to further your mutual interests, so that you can get along with people as well as function productively.

The more rigidly ingrained an individual's behavior pattern is, the more difficulty that person will probably encounter in trying to change it. For example, an extremely passive Type IV person will probably find it harder to behave assertively than a Type I person who wants to stay in control but be a little more sensitive to others. A good starting point for personal changes is to identify the kinds of verbal and nonverbal communication barriers you might be throwing in others' path to mutual understanding. In gaining an appreciation of the amount of commitment and effort involved in changing your own behavior, you also will learn more about influencing change in the behavior of others.

While these tasks may seem formidable, they are possible to achieve! Many people have found that, by making a conscious commitment and by persevering in their efforts to understand and apply new ways of interacting, they can actually cope more effectively with their own difficult customers.

## FOUR OPTIONS

Remember that everyone is someone else's difficult customer. Regardless of one's status relative to other people, each individual is responsible for his or her own attitudes, feelings and actions toward others. You have a choice when it comes to responding, although you are not always consciously aware of your options. You can choose to:

1. Preserve the status quo; that is, do nothing except continue to endure and gripe about the current situation;
2. Leave the situation, having decided that a solution to the problem is either impossible or not worth the drain on your time and energy;
3. Adjust your attitude; that is, view the problem from a different perspective (for example, by seeing the problem as residing in the interaction rather than in either of the persons themselves, or by refusing to take the other person's behavior so seriously or as a personal attack); or
4. Change your own behavior; in effect, this means interrupting an ineffective, unsatisfactory communication pattern, and replacing it with one that is more effective and potentially more satisfying. If you behave differently from your usual pattern, and *persist* in this new behavior over time, your difficult customers will eventually have to do something different in turn to cope with you.

Of these four choices, changing your own behavior, plus changing your perspective or attitude, represents the best hope of both taking care of your own needs and influencing the difficult people in your life to do something different themselves.

# DEALING EFFECTIVELY WITH DIFFICULT CUSTOMERS

Since behavioral change truly begins at home, with yourself, the first step towards dealing more effectively with others is to decide what you want to change. While this may sound like an overstatement of the obvious, many people do not know what they want. They know they would like to feel better about themselves and other people, more secure, more comfortable, more in control, happier, and so on. But they seldom take the time to envision what the ideal outcomes of their interactions would actually look like, sound like, and feel like. Instead, they engage in wishful thinking, along the lines of, "I wish I wasn't such a coward," or "If only she wasn't so defensive," or "Why does he have to be right all the time?"

Knowing what you don't want is not enough to get what you want. In fact, by constantly complaining to others about the negatives in your life and wishing that they would disappear, you may be engaging in a form of passive behavior that others find difficult to deal with. If you know only what you don't want, you will probably keep on getting it until you begin to envision some concrete, positive goals for yourself. Unless you have a vision of what you want, you probably won't get it. You have to be able to envision how things could be better, what you will actually do and say, how you will look, sound, and feel. That is the essence of hope and optimism. If you are chronically pessimistic, it is like a dam in the river of the evolution of human development. You have to be able to take the risk of visualizing how it could be. Then you have to be able to sustain the vision. Otherwise it is just wishful thinking, which drains your hope and self-esteem.

Each of you have the capacity as human beings to embark upon a heroic journey if only you hear the call to adventure and accept the challenge. The triumph of the human spirit depends upon your decision to persist in changing your communication patterns despite the impediments of your personal histories. The journey will eventually bring you full circle, back to where you started—yourself. But you will be stronger, more confident, and more effective. As the ancient Chinese saying goes, the journey of one thousand miles begins with a single step: Know what you want.

Achieving the vision entails not only persistence in making changes in your behavior but also recognition of those changes as they occur over time. In this respect, changing your behavior with difficult strangers is often easier and takes less time than changing your interactions with people who know you. The people you live or work with have had time to form a mental image of your personality—who you are and how you act. Difficult relationships *do not suddenly change* as a result of a one-time attempt at something new on your part. However, by paying attention and consistently applying the new behavior, you will begin to notice gradual changes in other people's behavior as they adjust to the new messages you are communicating.

Above all, for long-term behavioral change to occur, you must make a long-term commitment to sustain your vision of behavioral change without apology or regret, despite the inevitable obstacles and through times when the process seems endless. Without vision, failure is virtually guaranteed. Without long-term commitment, you will not only fail but resent the wasted time and energy.

For your vision of change to withstand the ups and downs of human interaction, you will have to be flexible, as well as persistent. Flexibility of body is a sign of physical health and strength. Flexibility in attitude and behavior is a sign of mental health and emotional strength. Remember that rigid behavioral patterns are what cause people difficulty in their relationships to begin with. If a new strategy doesn't seem to be working with a particular person, perhaps you need to go back and listen to the person more carefully, observing what is going on in yourself, the other, and the interaction. A more effective strategy will probably suggest itself. Being flexible also means being willing to give yourself and the other person the benefit of the doubt—for example, acknowledging that you or the other individual, for reasons outside of your relationship, may be in a bad mood or simply having a bad day.

One way of pumping up your self-confidence to meet your commitment is to adopt a more heroic identity for yourself, a persona or alter ego whose assertiveness and courage people can admire and that will at least help you function more assertively and courageously until you actually feel that way. For example, in the Arthurian legend, Perceval starts out a feckless and humble peasant boy on an adventure, but by putting on the armor of the Red Knight, he eventually becomes the hero who finds the Holy Grail! In other words, you must often "fake it until you make it!"

Another highly recommended method for maintaining vision and commitment to change is to identify people whom you can depend on for support during the process. Find someone you know who is not one of your difficult customers, someone who seems to care about you and with whom you can communicate easily and openly. This might be a spouse, a friend, or a co-worker. Tell that person about your decision to make some changes in your behavior and ask him or her to give you moral support in your venture. Do not expect the person to open doors or remove obstacles in your path like some legendary magician or fairy godmother. Do not expect him or her to take on any other responsibility for your changes other than to be there for you and to listen when you need to talk. Offer your support in return.

Creating this kind of mutually supportive relationship with a potential ally accomplishes a number of purposes, all of which are beneficial to you both. First, you no longer have to bear your burden of change alone. Second, your relationship with your ally is bound to become closer and stronger. Third, your friend will experience the joy and satisfaction that flow from the act of making someone else's life easier and happier. Whether you succeed or fail in dealing more effectively with your difficult people, the time and effort you invest in strengthening the bonds of mutual support and friendship will never be wasted. Indeed, the extent to which you can bridge the interpersonal gap between yourself and those to whom you feel closest, and work with them to accomplish something, is an excellent indicator of your potential ability to communicate and find a common ground with your difficult customers.

# References

1. For excellent advice and assistance in understanding and coping with people who exhibit symptoms of severe mental illness or pose the threat of danger to themselves and others in the library, see: Charles A. Salter and Jeffrey L. Salter, *On the Frontlines: Coping with the Library's Problem Patrons* (Englewood, CO: Libraries Unlimited, 1988).

# 3 COMMUNICATING WITH THE DIFFICULT CUSTOMER

Rather than allowing conflicting goals and styles to push us off balance, our task is to discover what we and the difficult person share *in common*, what we can agree upon, what we can both relate to, and what we can use to build goodwill and cooperation in achieving common objectives. In most instances, we are used to seeing the differences rather than the similarities between ourselves and our difficult customers. While it may be true that we are different from these people in many ways, it is also true that the more we focus on our differences, or on what we don't want, the more likely those differences will be magnified, the more likely there will be friction between us, and the less likely we will be inclined to cooperate with each other. Many marriages fail because of "irreconcilable differences" that at first seemed minor but became magnified and intensified over time. On the other hand, people in successful, cooperative relationships emphasize and build upon the experiences and intentions that they share in common, including their willingness to "agreeably disagree" from time to time.

Therefore, our first objectives in communicating more effectively with a difficult customer are to establish a common ground for understanding and to minimize the distance and difference between us. Rick Brinkman and Rick Kirschner, in their workshop on dealing with difficult people, refer to this basic communication skill as "pacing."[1] Others call it "active listening" or "empathic listening." Whatever the label, the process is what happens automatically when you are sharing an experience with someone you love and trust, or when you and another person are on the same wavelength. Much of the difference we perceive between ourselves and our difficult customers is the result either of interacting at a different pace or of conflicting needs and intentions (different personal agendas).

## NON-VERBAL COMMUNICATION

In the past quarter century, there has been a tremendous amount of research in the area of interpersonal communication. What investigators have found is that *nonverbal* behaviors bear the lion's share of the messages we communicate to others, like the musical setting of a song. Estimates vary, but most experts agree that people tend to respond to body language (facial expressions, eye contact, postures, and hand movements) with far more intensity than they do to the verbal components of communication. The volume and tone of our voices communicate much more of our meaning than the words we use. However, verbal creatures that we are, we tend to give most of our conscious attention to the words we hear, overlooking the three-fourths or more of the message that are contained in nonverbal behavior or vocal characteristics.

## WHAT YOU SEE (AND HEAR) IS WHAT YOU GET

If we were to unobtrusively observe the nonverbal communication of people who are in long-term caring relationships with each other, we would find that, more often than not, they tend to reflect each other's nonverbal behavior. This mirroring is not copy-cat imitation; that is, immediately doing exactly the same thing the other person does. Rather, it is a more subtle, unconscious adoption of one person's general deportment by the other during the course of the conversation. This kind of nonverbal mirroring is a way of communicating that the people are on common ground, that they are sharing a common experience with each other. When people do not reflect each other's body language, tone, and volume, their behavior tends to accentuate, rather than minimize, the differences between them. For example, if you normally greet people with a smile, and they reciprocate by smiling, you feel closer to them. If the other person is feeling angry, fearful, or depressed and does not return your smile, you can put this nonverbal information to work for you. If you wish to stay connected to this person, and not alienate him or her, continued smiling on your part would be inappropriate. Instead, you would change your facial expression and body movements to express concern and the desire to help, again decreasing the perceived differences and emotional distance between you.

### Sharing Common Experience

The things we share in common are the basis of mutual respect and understanding. For example, we all share common needs, desires, and experiences, although they vary in degree. Our common dreams, ideals, and values draw us together. The differences between us can be the basis either of conflict, if we dwell excessively on them, or of delight, if we focus on our common ground while exploring each other's uniqueness. It is a matter of perspective and focus.

We are in the world to grow, to learn, to love, and (in libraries) to serve. We accomplish all of these purposes by extending ourselves beyond our current boundaries, whether they are physical, mental, or spiritual. We are individuals, to be sure. But while each of us is unique, we have much in common, and few of us would survive for long without the concern and cooperation of others. As human beings, we have a natural inclination to connect with others. The things we share in common draw us together. Our individual uniqueness can be a source of wonder, exploration, delight, and growth for others.

### Body Language

The reflection of body language lets people know if we are friend or foe, for or against them. If we move at the same speed and use the same kinds of body postures, facial expressions, and gestures as they, we indicate that we are ready to cooperate, and that we are seeking a "win-win" outcome. If our body language is different, it signals a competitive, "win-lose" motivation. If we believe someone is against us, it is highly unlikely for us to want to risk cooperating with them. This does not necessarily make us difficult people. However, if one person is perceived by the other as an opponent, the differences between them may push them further into behaving in more difficult ways.

Again, the goals of effective communication are to move toward a common understanding and to minimize, not exacerbate, differences. We need to break down the defensive barriers that differences impose between us, and communicate a message of cooperation and mutuality. If this is what we want, and we know it, we must be willing to make a conscious effort to adapt our body language to that of the difficult person, while paying attention as well to what they are saying.

### Speech Patterns

Loud, fast music can get us on our feet and moving, while soft, slow music can relax us to the point of drowsiness. In like manner, the human voice, depending on its tone, pace, and volume, has the power to calm us, persuade us, or even incite us to violence. Only about 20 percent of our spoken message is conveyed by the words we speak. The rest is communicated by the voice.

Often we can tell a lot about how a person thinks by observing how he or she talks. Some of us form our mental concepts in words; others think in pictures. Neither cognitive style is superior to the other. People simply vary in the ways they acquire and process information. Some people tend to learn more easily from things they see and less easily from things they only hear. They see instant pictures in their minds and describe them to others. Others process information more linearly, in words, phrases, and sentences, and they repeat these for others to hear. In a learning situation, for example, some people can listen to a sound recording of a lecture and follow the speaker's train of thought quite handily. The more visually oriented learners will respond better to a video recording or to the lecturer's presence, especially if the speaker uses illustrations such as charts and graphs. A multimedia approach is probably a speaker's best bet for any type of group presentation, since most of us take in information through both eyes *and* ears although to different degrees of effectiveness.

Since human beings can think much faster than they can speak, we can reasonably conclude that people who typically talk very fast are probably more visual in their thinking. They use words to describe the pictures in their minds as fast as they can flip through them. People who think in verbal concepts, on the other hand, tend to speak more slowly, because of the more linear, sequential nature of language. A slow-talker may have difficulty keeping up with a fast-talking, more visual thinker and may feel overwhelmed by the pace. By the same token, the faster-talker's attention may begin to stray if the slower-talker's words are too abstract or not descriptive enough to paint a visual picture in the fast-talker's mind.

Although one style may be more dominant than the other, we all possess the capacity to think both visually and linearly. However, awareness of the other person's dominant cognitive style can assist us in communicating with him or her. For example, if we know that our normal pace is faster than the other person's, we can slow down our tempo and allow him or her to keep up with us. If we are more slow-talking, we will probably have to increase our tempo to get the other person on the same track as us. We might also use more descriptive or metaphorical language with him or her or even literally draw pictures or diagrams to keep the person focused on what we are saying.

Our ability to get the attention and cooperation of others is one measure of our personal power. The whole point of initiating interactions with others is to get them to understand our needs and intentions and enlist their cooperation in fulfilling them. When we know what we need and want, our next step is to get it. As human beings, however, we exist within a social context. We need the cooperation of others to get what we need and want. When other people cooperate, they help us to fulfill our desires and intentions. However, cooperation is a two-way proposition. The social contract is reciprocal; that is, if our relationships with people are to be truly cooperative, we must be willing to help others meet *their* particular needs and wants at the same time they help us. This is why it is so important to adjust the tempo of our voice and our movements to the other person's speed and rhythms. It minimizes differences and builds mutual understanding that, in turn, leads to cooperation and collaboration. The more we can reduce perceived differences, the more likely we are to get cooperation, and the less likely we are to experience conflict with our difficult customers or, for that matter, anyone.

There are some people whose voices are naturally loud and/or intrusive, who tend to be heard above the voices of others whether or not they are being aggressive. However, many of us associate a raised voice with anger and aggression. Therefore, another useful technique for building cooperation with people is to subtly vary the decibel level of our voice to match theirs. This means that if another person is being aggressive and trying to overpower us by raising his or her voice or shouting, we need to respond by becoming more assertive in our own behavior. From our childhood, many of us, particularly females, have learned to respond to aggressive behavior by becoming quieter and more submissive. When we were small, others (both children and adults) whose physical size and strength were greater than our own posed a very real threat to our safety, especially when these people were competitive, hostile, or aggressive. We learned to avoid danger by either running away or capitulating to the more powerful individual.

# HOW TO BEHAVE WITH ASSERTIVENESS

As a grown up, you may carry these learned behaviors into your adult interactions. However, as adults, these are neither your only options nor the most effective. They may, in fact, prompt the other person either to discount you as weak or literally not to see you at all! Your instinctive or learned tendency to *underplay* another's aggression is inherently wise, since it helps you to maintain control of your own behavior and stops you from adding fuel to the fire. However, withdrawing or submitting to another's aggressiveness is *not* the most effective behavior for getting your own needs and wants met, beyond the need to escape physical harm.

Bear in mind that there *are* situations in which other people really do pose a physical threat to you, and in which fleeing the situation is the most appropriate response. However, these dangerous situations are not the ones being discussed here. Rather, we are talking about interactions with people who use their physical presence and the loudness of their voices to overwhelm us. In these instances, if you want the other person to stop competing and start cooperating, you will have to stand up to them. This means literally standing up if the other person is standing, and *increasing* the decibel level of your voice rather than lowering it. This does not mean trying to match their aggressiveness by shouting them down or hurling verbal counterattacks. Your intensity level should underplay the customer's aggressiveness without compromising your stance.

Remember, the closer you move towards the other person in your body language and vocal responses, the less different you appear to them. Unless you are in real physical danger, this assertive behavior is far more effective than moving to a position in which the other person perceives you as weak. Assertively mirroring the other person's volume and staying at the same eye-level with him or her, without matching his or her hostile attitude, accomplishes two objectives:

1. The other person is more likely to move away from an extremely aggressive position and toward your more assertive one (in other words, closer to you).
2. The other person is more likely to respect your strength, as displayed in your assertive behavior, and less likely to see you as a weakling who can be easily overcome.

Both of these outcomes reduce the perceived differences between you and expand your common ground. They allow you both to exercise personal power and to maintain some measure of control in the interaction.

## POWER AND CONTROL

The concepts of power and control, although related, should not be confused. *Power* means the ability to get others to cooperate with you so that you can get what you need and want. Ideally it is the win-win position. *Control* means "being in charge of what I am able to be in charge of." It is the ability to choose the direction and the intensity of *one's own behavior*. People often use the terms power and control to describe what is really weakness and desperation. It is weakness when people are not able to get cooperation. It is desperation when they substitute manipulation or coercion of others for an inability to choose among other positive behavioral options. Viewed from this perspective, they are relatively powerless and out of control.

To be assertive is to stand up and speak up when someone is being aggressive and to adopt a win-win attitude, not a competitive, win-lose attitude, which emphasizes differences. The true power and control position is one that moves in the direction of the other person, both literally and figuratively, empowering both of you to meet somewhere in the middle, on a common ground.

## UNDERSTANDING THE CONCEPTS

Although the difficult customer's needs and intentions may often get lost in the difficult behavior that delivers it, they are the reasons behind the behavior in the first place. If you are to understand, you must listen with the purpose of understanding. Understanding, in this context, means empathic listening—that is, understanding as the other person understands. The meaning you are striving for is the *difficult customer's* meaning, which is not necessarily what you would mean if you used the same words. Active, empathic listening is the easiest way to let other people know that they have your attention and that what they said has been heard. It may be the most valuable gift you can ever give to anyone. In addition to reflection of body language and voice, you can move toward understanding, and buy yourself more time to respond, by:

1. repeating back what the other person says, and
2. asking questions that will help the person explain exactly what he or she means.

## VERBAL REFLECTION

When you restate what the person has said, it does not have to be an exact word-for-word, "parrot" style, restatement. On the other hand, for the novice, using many of the same words can be a useful way to begin practicing this skill. Remember that the goal is understanding, not interpretation or even perfection of the technique. Verbal and non-verbal reflection are the first steps toward understanding but not synonymous with it. They let the difficult customer know that you are listening and that you have heard what they have said. They also let people know that you respect and trust them enough to let *them* take the conversational lead for the time being. They convey the idea that you are willing to meet them more than halfway, that you are not there to add confusion or defensiveness but to continue listening. For example, in the case of the tardy spouse in Chapter 1:

> Spouse A: You need time to relax? What about me? This is the third time in a month I'll have to make excuses for you to my parents. And I was really looking forward to this evening. By the time we get there, the evening will be practically shot! And all because of you and that antique you're so sentimental about!

Spouse A is upset at Spouse B's late arrival. Spouse B has narrowly escaped an accident while driving home in an increasingly unreliable car. B might continue in a defensive vein, defending the car and himself and fighting at cross-purposes with A. On the other hand, if B were to pause for a moment, then shift into verbal and nonverbal reflection, he might choose temporarily to overlook the "dig" about his affection for the car and say something like, "I can see how frustrating this is for you! I keep showing up late, and you have to keep making excuses for keeping your parents waiting!" Notice that B is not apologizing, counterattacking, or defending. B is simply providing A with some verbal reflection and feedback, letting her know that she has been heard and that what she has said is important to B. At this point, B may not fully understand or see things as A sees them, but what B says tells A that understanding and cooperation are more important than winning the argument.

# EXPLORING THE SPECIFICS

The next step in communicating with empathy is to find out exactly what is going on with the other person. You can obtain clarification by asking open-ended questions that begin with *who, what, where, when,* and *how.* This allows him or her to provide specific information that will help you more fully understand. (For this reason, it is not a good idea to ask *why* questions at this point in the interaction, especially if the other person already appears to be acting defensive. It is very common for a difficult customer to translate "why" as "you should" or "you shouldn't"; that is, as a *judgment* instead of as an attempt to understand.)

People often get into trouble with their difficult customers because they and/or their customers think they understand what they are talking about when they really don't. Rather than check out your assumptions, you simply respond as if they really meant what you *thought* they meant. For example, if the other person says, "I need that information as soon as possible," you might assume that the need is both important and urgent. Depending on the perceived power and authority you assign to the other person, you might drop everything and spend the next hour compiling as much information as you can in whatever format is expected. On the other hand, you might assume that the request is neither all that important nor all that urgent, that this is just the person's way of trying to impress you. People often complicate matters by giving very little information to start with. (After all, *I* know what I mean, why doesn't everybody else?) It is precisely at times like this, when you think you know what the other person is talking about, that you ought to ask questions like, "Who (which person) is going to be using it?" "What specific information is needed?" "What kind of format is acceptable?" (Brief outline? Specific facts? A lengthy formal report? A collection of articles? A bibliography?) "When you say 'as soon as possible,' what does that mean?" (In five minutes? By lunch time? By the end of the week?) "When is your deadline?" "Where do you need it to be delivered?" ("Or will you be picking it up?") "Would a phone call be alright, or do you need hard copy?" If you do not understand an answer to one or more of these questions, step back and again use verbal reflection (e.g., "Your deadline is Friday at noon. Does that mean you need the information by then, or you need to have your project done by then? What is your deadline for receiving the information in time to use it?"). Although these journalistic kinds of questions are part of good reference interviews, it is also a good idea to ask them as a matter of course in many other library situations, not only with patrons but also with co-workers and supervisors. Fact-based questions like these are another way of signaling to others that you are trying to understand the problem or situation as *they* see it, and that your intention is to cooperate with them to find a solution. They reduce confusion, doubts, and fears about possible misunderstandings and prevent wasted time and anxiety. Asking clarifying questions also helps people to get beyond the urgency and emotion of the current moment and to focus on exploring the problem in more detail (with the listener as friendly collaborator).

By asking for specific information, you will uncover details that neither you nor they may have been aware of before, some aspects of a problem, for instance, that may have prevented a particular solution from working effectively. With the details on the table for you to examine, there is room for negotiation, compromise, and agreement on a mutually acceptable solution.

## KNOWING WHAT YOU WANT AND SAYING SO

You can model the basic skills of nonverbal and verbal reflection to meet a person's need to be heard (both content and process), and explore the specifics by asking fact-seeking questions that build a common ground of understanding.

Part of the problem with difficult customers, however, is that they often lack very basic communication skills. They cannot reasonably be expected to reciprocate your efforts to practice them. Once you have worked your way through the defensiveness and emotional distance between yourself and the other person, therefore, it is equally important that you communicate your own needs and positive intentions clearly and directly. Again, in order to do this, you must know what you want: what your goals are. It is unfortunate but true that, in many dysfunctional conversations, both parties start out with virtually identical intentions but neglect to acknowledge and communicate them. Take the case of Spouse A and Spouse B, for example. A and B were both looking forward to spending some pleasant time together with A's parents. Both A and B are feeling disappointed, annoyed, frustrated, and unappreciated. They have so much in common, yet they fail to acknowledge it. Instead of drawing them together, their interaction polarizes them. Suppose B were to respond differently to A's accusation, "We were due at Mother and Dad's a half hour ago! You could have at least called and let me know you were going to be late!"? Rather than defensively responding " . . . Besides, your parents won't mind if we're a little late," suppose B were to say something like, "Gee, honey, I'm really disappointed about this, too. I really enjoy relaxing with your folks. They've done so much for us and I hate being late so often lately. We really need to replace that old car. Let's talk it over with your parents tonight. What do you say?" *Before:* A is feeling discounted and (on behalf of her parents) unappreciated. *After:* A knows that B cares about her feelings and appreciates all that her parents do for them. *The difference:* B is aware of what he really wants and communicates his positive intentions clearly and directly. This reminds A that her own needs and intentions are virtually the same as B's and disposes her to work *with* her partner, B, to solve the current problem and prevent its recurrence. Their relationship grows in strength and mutuality, too.

In summary, the key to effective interpersonal communication is making a personal commitment to:

1. know what you want (your *positive* intention) and ask for it;
2. pay attention to the verbal and nonverbal messages that others communicate and reflect them verbally and nonverbally;
3. ask questions that build understanding of others' needs and intentions;
4. be assertive about finding and expanding the common ground you share with others.

Change must begin with you. All you can reasonably hope for from your difficult customers is the possibility that, given time and your example, they might also be willing to change their own difficult behavior patterns.

# References

1. Rick Brinkman and Rick Kirschner, *How to Deal with Difficult People* (videocassette) Vol. I, 74 min., Career Track, 1988.

# 4 UNDERSTANDING AND DEALING WITH ANGER

What is this thing called anger and why devote a full chapter to it? Don't we get enough of it on the evening news? There's so much anger and violence in the world, in our community, even in our families! Why can't people be nice to each other or, at least, just live and let live? Where does anger come from? Is it *ever* appropriate to express it, or is it always one of the "seven deadlies"? Is it even possible to handle anger in a way that *everyone* can win?

In this chapter we will explore the many manifestations of a troublesome emotion that produces more stress and anxiety in library staff than any other: anger.

Imagine the following scenario:

Jane, red-faced and angry, enters the branch public library one Friday afternoon at about 5:20 p.m. and walks determinedly to the circulation desk. There are two staff members on duty at the desk, one of whom, Mike, is charging out materials to a middle-aged woman and her five-year-old grandson. The other staff member, Mary, is busily tidying up the work area before the library closes at 5:30 for the weekend. Monday is a holiday, the library will be closed until Tuesday morning, and Mary is looking forward to the extra day off and a chance to catch up with her garden and her own grandchildren. She sees Jane approaching the desk, and while she is still thinking to herself, "Uh oh. This looks like trouble coming," Jane loudly demands an explanation for the sheet of paper she is waving in Mary's face.

"I'm furious," Jane sputters. "I just got home from a week-long business trip, and I'm sitting down to relax and go through the mail, when the first thing staring me in the face is this 'bill' for a book you people *claim* is four months overdue. I never took this book out. I never even heard of it. How *dare* you bill me for some book I've never even heard of? Why, I've never even had a book overdue more than two days in my life, let alone lost one. This is an insult! I work hard and I pay taxes to support this library. I think I'm entitled to a little respect. But, no, all I get is a hassle. You people better get your act together. And don't expect me to vote for that bond issue you're pushing. I have better things to do with my time and money than waste it on the library!"

Along with Jane's shouting, Mary is aware of the grandmother's attempt to hurry her grandchild away from the commotion and out the door. Meanwhile, Mike has retreated to safety in the circulation office behind the desk, leaving Mary alone to deal with Jane's wrathful outburst.

If you were Mary, how would you respond to Jane's "in your face" behavior? Do you have difficulty dealing with hostile people, the ones who express anger aggressively? Would you be tempted to label Jane a problem patron?

## LABELS AND CHANGE

Before we discuss the process and content of anger, it is useful at this point to repeat our basic premise about the classification of emotions and behavior. Remember that, in this book, we are attempting to understand and deal with interpersonal difficulty by examining and categorizing behavior, and by trying more effective responses, not by labeling and categorizing persons. Characterizing people in terms of "types"—that is, in terms of fixed notions of values, ideas, attitudes, and personality traits—by labeling them in accordance with one or a few aspects of their behavior, can save time and energy in the short run because it allows us to short-circuit our thinking to some extent. Labels can give us a quick and easy handle on a person's behavior. But they can also be ineffective or even counterproductive if we use the label as a substitute for thinking. A label, if misused globally to define a person, may actually divert our attention from the actual person to a false sense of understanding.

Labels, like slogans, are seductive. They can deceive us into thinking that we have a total picture of a person's thoughts and actions, past and present, and a complete set of expectations about how that person will behave in the future, without having to actually find out for ourselves. In other words, labeling persons as difficult or problem customers or employees is a convenient way of fitting people into stereotypes, and gives us convenient, but stereotypical ways of interpreting the meaning of their behavior, along with stereotypical expectations of how they will behave in the future.

The problem is that people are not one-dimensional, and the circumstances that surround interactions are never exactly the same. Individuals never completely conform to the preconceived stereotypes that our labels want to force them into. The fact is that people can learn, and they are capable of changing their behavior, either through their own initiative or in adaptation to changes in others' behavior. While some authors have used catchy labels (e.g., "tanks," "snipers," etc.) to distinguish general types of difficult behavior, it is extremely important to bear in mind that labels themselves are simply *models*.

Again, the model is a way of describing, understanding, and (sometimes) predicting behavior. The model can help one to develop coping strategies. But the model is never more than an abstraction based on selected parameters or dimensions of real situations. We can never fully define people by our models or typologies, no matter how useful they can be. We cannot change other people's behavior merely by labeling them and their behavior as difficult. Real change in our interactions springs primarily from the fact that we can change our own behavior and from the hope that other people might eventually choose change in response.

## ANGER IS NOT A FOUR-LETTER WORD

Anger is more than a feeling. It is a natural human emotion that we all experience. It involves both physical reactions and mental processes, including thoughts and interpretations of thoughts. It can be healthy or destructive. It is often related to aggression and hostility, but these concepts are not synonymous with each other or with anger. When a person is angry, he or she may be consciously aware of the emotion or may unconsciously repress it. Many people have been taught, by example, by edict, or by experiences with important people in their formative years, that getting angry is wrong, immoral, or at least socially unacceptable. People may deny, both to themselves and to others, that they are angry and then act out their anger in indirect, more subtle ways. If denial is not possible, they may feel guilty about feeling angry and, at the same time, feel resentful toward the object of the anger.

Some people take the increasingly popular position that anger is not wrong in itself but must be released or expressed. The belief here is that if anger is not expressed when it occurs, the person, like a pressure cooker without a release valve, will experience dire consequences. Indeed, medical evidence suggests a connection between extreme or unrelenting stress and certain psychosomatic conditions, including ulcers, hypertension, and even some types of cancer. These people (and their doctors) may firmly believe that it is wrong or unhealthy not to blow off steam.

However, people do not live in isolation, but in the context of society. When anger is directed at or expressed in the presence of other people, there is a wide range of consequences depending largely on the content of the anger—what and whom it was about—and the process—*how* the person expressed it. The consequences (such as punishment or abandonment) of "letting it all hang out" in an outburst of temper whenever anger occurs are not always what the individual would choose. People in our society tend to feel anxious in the presence of another person's rage and are likely either to resist, to withdraw out of fear of involvement (e.g., Mike), or to retaliate in kind, even when they are not the target of the anger.

The emotional energy, the steam that generates and supports a sudden release of anger, is often contagious, even when the other person is merely a bystander, not the object of the anger. Close friends and family members are often more vulnerable to the contagious nature of a loved one's rage than a relative stranger, since their relationship already embodies strong emotional connections. If one's friend or relative is the target of an angry outburst, he or she might respond, even retaliate, much more strongly than a stranger would. If the friend is merely a witness to an expression of anger directed elsewhere, there may be a strong temptation to sympathize with the angry person, perhaps even to provide more fuel for the fire, in a misguided but sincere effort to help the angry person feel better.

# UNDERSTANDING ANGER

A journalistic approach to anger and other emotions is a simple, yet effective method of understanding how our own feelings work within us, how we behave under their influence, and how we might come to terms with them. A reporter seeking the facts of a story will ask, "Who?", "What?", "Where?", "When?", "How?", (and sometimes) "Why?" to gain understanding of the incident. Researchers basically ask these same questions to understand concepts and solve problems. Adapting this systematic investigative approach to the study of our own thoughts, emotions, and behavior, we can see that as individuals we have different styles of behaving when we are angry and different ways of talking about it.

Given that anger does not just appear from out of the blue and strike us unaware, where does anger come from? What makes you angry? Is it other people's crazy behavior? Bureaucratic red tape? Is it a group that you dislike? If so, is the group also different from you in some critical way (e.g., by race, gender, age, or class)? Is it your children who make you angry? Your parents? Rich people?

Poor people? Men? Women? Once you have identified the people or groups that are the primary catalysts of your anger, ask yourself: What is it about them or the way they relate to me that triggers my anger?

Many people feel uncomfortable, even fearful, in the presence of others who are physically different from themselves, although they do not necessarily feel angry toward them. Often this discomfort springs from internalized stereotypes learned from growing up in a society with historic and endemic notions of racism, sexism, classism, etc., that results in members of one group perceiving members of another group almost automatically as "the enemy." We learn to perceive these people as a threat against whom we must be prepared to defend ourselves. Beyond these isms, however, we sometimes feel angry, not merely because we perceive another person as different, but because the person's difference and behavior conveys an inequality of worth or power. In other words, we become angry because we perceive the other person as unjust, contemptuous, rude, insulting, patronizing, or condescending, which places us in a relatively inferior position to them. On the other hand, we can also feel anger in response to another person's inferior position and passive, subservient behavior. (Among socioeconomic classes, this is known as "blaming the victim.")

In its milder forms, anger can be intense but short-term—for example, in response to a stranger's bad manners or violations of social etiquette in a grocery check-out line, in a theater, or in traffic. In its more serious forms, anger can be long-term and chronic—for example, in response to being victimized, betrayed, or abandoned by a spouse, a parent, or someone who was or is important to us. Either way, we tend to respond to these violations of our psychological boundaries, our written or unwritten social rules, first with *shock and denial* ("This can't be happening!"), then *confusion*, as we become energized to respond ("How could this have happened?"), and finally *anger* ("How dare they do this to me!"). Keep in mind that so far we are only describing *internal* responses to a perceived injustice or violation, not our external behavior, which will be addressed next.

What do you *do* when you are angry? The answer to this "what" question generally depends on one's perceived status or power in the relationship, our perceptions of the probable consequences of expressing anger, and the relative value we place on the potential rewards of expressing anger (e.g., restoration of justice or our personal boundaries) versus the potential negative consequences (e.g., retaliation or continued ill will). Does each of us see the other as our equal? Or is one of us in a superior or inferior position in terms of perceived personal power or position? For example: "I just don't get it. I go in for my annual performance review, and instead of getting rated on my *performance*, I get other people's out-of-context comments, innuendos, and gossip dumped on me. She says *I* have a bad attitude. She doesn't manage people—she just jerks people around! I hate this place! I wish I could just walk in there and quit!" Is it "safe" to express this anger directly? Or must it be suppressed, expressed indirectly, or redirected back upon ourselves or another, safer object?

We hardly ever have time to consider these variables once we are already angry. Most people react spontaneously in these circumstances. The varieties of behavior we use to deal with our anger are infinite. Some people scream and shout. Some people use (or abuse) food, alcohol, or other substances to alter their angry mood. Some talk to anyone and everyone except the target, repeatedly going over and over the incident that made them angry, reliving it again and again, maintaining their anger without resolution. Some withdraw to pout, sulk, and otherwise punish the offender with noncommunication. Some people blame themselves in a co-dependent sort of way. Some people write angry letters and send them to their targets or to people who have power to punish their targets.

Many people physically displace their anger—for example, by beating up a pillow or taking it out on a racquetball. Others may feel angry at the boss, then go home and kick the dog or scream at their children. Some people (many of us, really) carry childhood anger at parents and authority figures with them into adulthood, and take it out on people they currently perceive as having control or authority over them. Sabotage, sarcasm, and other forms of back-stabbing are common ways of expressing anger without confronting the target directly. Note that the consequences of these behaviors vary as much as the behaviors themselves, and that the consequences are largely beyond our control.

# DEALING CONSTRUCTIVELY WITH ANGER

In contrast to the less-than-productive behaviors described above, some people have learned to deal with their anger by consciously analyzing their characteristic triggers and responses to anger *when they are not angry*. As a result, they have learned behaviors that allow them to get rid of the anger while minimizing the negative consequences to themselves. For example, some people have trained themselves to relax through meditation, nonaggressive exercise, reading, or distracting themselves in other ways. They count to a hundred (or a thousand), deep breathe, or take a walk around the block to calm themselves before deciding either how to respond, or whether an angry response is worth the possible consequences.

Others get their anger out by writing letters to their offenders, and then destroying the letters! The very act of writing can help us step back from our anger by forcing us to consciously focus our thoughts. Seeing our anger (or any of our troublesome emotions) on paper in a letter or a journal allows us to gain distance and perspective on events and problems and permits more creative, productive solutions to emerge. It also allows us time to cool off, to let some of the emotional energy dissipate (the mental analog to punching a pillow), and prevents us from recklessly doing and saying things we don't really mean and might regret later. It keeps us from overreacting and exaggerating events out of proportion. Through self-examination, we can identify our specific anger buttons; that is, the ideas, themes, words, labels, perceptions, conclusions, expressions, mannerisms, or actions that set us off.

Some people have developed both the skill and the fortitude to accept their own limitations and those of their environment, and to make rational, calm, statements about their anger directly to the appropriate target. These people are willing to stop generalizing and assigning blame and start seeing others' intentions and behavior in a more positive light. They are willing to move through and beyond their own and others' anger in order to explore common needs and intentions and to seek collaborative solutions. They are willing to accept the consequences of their successes or failures. Unfortunately, these role models are all too rare in a society that rewards and seems almost addicted to competitive and destructive forms of anger.

To further understand and expand the options for dealing with your own anger, you might want to write down your answer to the following question: What objective(s) does my expression of anger accomplish for me? Your answers may vary widely, but there will be common elements. For many people, expressing anger makes them feel empowered and in control of their situation, assertive rather than passive and victimized. Balance is restored to the scales of justice, as cherished personal values, attitudes, and beliefs are defended and protected from attack. They are not out to destroy their enemies; rather, their goal is a resolution that is mutually satisfying. In contrast, other people may have learned that the expression of anger, especially in a hostile or an aggressive way, allows them to win—that is, to have their own way—but if they are to win, the other has to lose.

This latter understanding of anger as a weapon of aggression and victory is often confused with the concept of anger as a naturally energizing human emotion, a process over which you can exert some rational control, the idea being emphasized in this chapter. The following working definition should clarify and distinguish this concept:

> *Anger* refers to an emotion that is accompanied by a rush of emotional energy and has a number of components. The physical or bodily characteristics of anger that people experience when angry are practically identical to the "fight-or-flight" phenomena experienced by prehistoric men and women, including sweaty palms, a pounding heart, and a pouring of adrenalin into the system to prepare the body to take action to defend itself against a challenge or to escape danger. While the physical symptoms are the most observable aspect of anger, the mind, or perceptual component of anger, is at least as important.

Think of a situation with another person in which you were feeling angry, only to experience a change of feeling when you discovered new information. For example, suppose you are seated on a crowded bus, trying to concentrate on your reading to pass the time. You have had an irritating day, and the bus ride home is hot and uncomfortable. Suddenly a man working his way down the aisle steps squarely and heavily on your foot. You react with shock, then the awareness that something painful has happened, and then with anger at the thoughtless injustice perpetrated upon you. Just as you are about to snap, "Why don't you watch where you're going?", you see the man's white cane and realize that he is blind. Your anger disappears almost instantly, and you spring into action, not to fight back but to offer the man your seat! Your irritable mood changes to one of concern. Your emotion changes from anger to shame, then to concern and compassion.

The emotion changed because your perception changed. The foot-stomping event did not directly cause your anger; your interpretation of the event as a careless intrusion upon your personal boundaries brought forth anger. A change occurred in the interpretation of the event, and your discovery of the man's inability to see changed your emotional response.

Anger and all other emotions occur in response to perceptions and your interpretations of them. The key to being in control of your emotional expressions is realization that emotions depend largely on how you perceive, translate, and interpret the content of any interpersonal situation. This is true for both difficult and non-difficult interactions. The locus of control lies in your attribution of responsibility. When you perceive that your success or comfort is due to your own work, you feel joy. When you perceive that success or comfort is due to luck, you might feel guilt or apprehension that someone will find out that you don't deserve the credit. When you perceive that your failure or discomfort is due to your own fault, you feel fear or worry that you might be blamed or punished. When you perceive that your failure or discomfort is due to others' fault, you feel anger.

The mind plays such an integral part in all of the emotions, which are many in number. Your complex mental faculties are able to process vast amounts of information in an instant. By now it should be clear that you are not limited to only one emotion at a time or to only one feeling about a given situation. You can have many feelings about the same event, at the same time or in succession, as your perspective and perceptions shift. You do not feel one way or the other but one way *and* the other. You choose, either consciously or unconsciously (perhaps out of habit), which emotion gets the spotlight of attention. It follows logically, therefore, that you can often change how you feel by changing what you choose to focus on. One of the most productive and rewarding personal challenges you can tackle in your life is that of sorting through your sometimes chaotic feelings and putting them in some kind of useful order (a natural for library-minded people!).

Once you understand that you have choices about which emotion will get your attention, it naturally follows that you have choices about which emotion you will express. Just as the expression of an emotion can vary, so can the potential consequences. In society, there seem to be a number of unwritten, unspoken norms about the way people deal with the expression of emotion. Americans frequently take things very personally, assuming that the expression of anger signals a hostile attitude and an intention to harm them, or that the expression of fear or hurt means passivity and helplessness, which are somehow more socially acceptable, especially in women. When you express fear or hurt, for example, it often evokes compassion and caring from others; when you express anger, it often triggers defense, withdrawal, or counterattack, even when the other person is not the target of the anger!

## DEFINING HOSTILITY AND AGGRESSION

Being angry is not the same as being rude, aggressive, or hostile, although many people in our society equate these terms:

> *Hostility* refers to an attitude rather than a feeling. It is characterized by dislike, distrust, cynicism, or envy directed at another person, group or institution. A person with a hostile attitude might wish evil on the other but may not necessarily be feeling angry at a given moment.

> *Aggression* is an action or behavior against another, performed with the intention of doing harm. It also is not necessarily associated with anger, although many people do behave aggressively when they feel angry. Many of us have experienced the direct or vicarious negative consequences of out-and-out aggression early and often enough in life that we don't usually behave aggressively when angry. Some of us fluctuate between open aggression and passive-aggression depending on how powerful we perceive the other person to be.

You can be angry without being aggressive. You can be angry without being hostile. You can be aggressive or hostile without being angry. You are responsible for your emotions, and you can choose how to express them or not express them.

Think about someone you would describe as slow to anger. What is it about this person's emotional persona that makes him or her different from another person who seems compelled to deal with the world in a cloud of hostile vigilance? People who go though life in a competitive mode, in which they believe there can only be one winner, tend to get angry often, especially when there is a strong fear of not coming out on top. More than likely, slow-to-anger persons have developed different ways of thinking about and responding to anger.

For example, they might react with humor instead of defensiveness, even when attacked. Note that we are not talking about witty sniping or sarcasm, which can appear humorous to onlookers, while being used to as a weapon to attack or counterattack. Genuine humor is a sign that the person understands just how absurd life can be, how unfair people are sometimes, and that the person has chosen not to take it personally. This choice does not deny that something is wrong; rather, it affirms that, while difficult, the situation is probably not catastrophic. The person who uses humor appropriately and successfully to deal with the other's anger has found another way of thinking about and explaining the other person's intentions and behavior.

Likewise, the person who can look at the other person's anger, and can see the hurt, fear, or frustration hidden under it, can often contain and diffuse the other's anger. Any time you look for an alternative interpretation of another's anger, before reacting in knee-jerk fashion, you open yourself to alternative responses that enable you to deflate your own anger and that of the other.

To summarize, what you believe and the way you think about a situation or another person's behavior largely determines how you feel. How you feel, and the intensity with which you feel, has an enormous impact on your behavior. How you behave in an emotionally charged interpersonal situation, depends to a great extent on what you believe to be the causes of your feelings, what you have been taught about those feelings, and how you have learned to act in emotional circumstances.

In the course of growing up in a certain family or culture, people learn to place a positive or negative value on anger. For example, in some families, anger is one of the "seven deadly sins," which lead to spiritual sickness and, according to some religious doctrines, merit eternal punishment. In other families, anger is viewed as a cultural expectation, a normal way of releasing energy and of connecting with other family members. The culture of anger is learned at home, in a sense. You learn what and whom should anger you and what and whom shouldn't. You learn how you are supposed to act when angry, and which expressions of anger are permitted, and under which circumstances.

You learn which expressions of anger will work for you and which will work against you, in terms of the consequences you experience. Some people learn to gradually escalate their angry tactics to resolve an issue; others learn to strike first and swiftly, then explain their anger calmly. The tactics chosen have much to do, again, with the perceived relative power of the persons involved. While you may have learned some inappropriate beliefs and behaviors about anger as you were growing up, it is often difficult to relearn more appropriate ones. The deeply ingrained lessons of childhood were taught by people who were perceived as possessing tremendous power to bestow or withhold love and to dispense rewards and punishment. Your adult experiences with people or institutions in positions of authority, with power to punish, or at least make life difficult for you, tend to reinforce earlier learning. Whether your perceptions of the other person's power are realistic or not, most people find it more difficult to express anger to people who appear to have the power to deliver harmful consequences.

What are you to do, then, when anger enters the interpersonal picture? The solution is two-pronged:

1. Study your own anger in order to understand it and to learn alternative responses.
2. Learn to distinguish the circumstances in which it is advantageous to express anger from those in which it is not.

# WHAT'S YOUR ANGER PROFILE?

An understanding of your own anger pattern (or other potentially troubling emotional patterns) is essential to changing your thinking and behavior. This understanding can be achieved by starting with a personal commitment to observe your own behavior and take personal responsibility for changing it. You should ask yourself, and write down your answers to, the following questions:

- Is my anger more extensive or intense in certain relationships than in others?
- If so, what is different about those relationships (e.g., perceived distribution of power, degree of intimacy, or emotional investment)?
- Is the anger with the person generalized (about a number of things), or is it concerned with something very specific?
- Is my anger part of some transition or phase of development I'm going through (e.g., grief due to loss or change, such as the death of a loved one, a new job, a geographical relocation, or an illness)?
- What do I hope to gain from being angry?
- How often and how intensely do I feel angry?
- How long does the anger last?
- What did I do when I was angry?
- Did I confront the target of my anger directly?
- Did I simply "rehearse" it with other people?

- Did I swallow it to avoid expressing it at all?
- Did the extent and intensity of my response correspond with that of the perceived offense?
- Was I too aggressive or too passive?
- Were we on the same "wavelength?"
- Did we focus on the common underlying problem between us or get distracted by appearances and surface issues?
- What did I gain?
- What did I lose?
- Did our communication improve or did it suffer?
- Did my self-esteem rise or fall?
- Did we solve the underlying problem or make it worse?
- Was there a win-win outcome, or was there a clear winner and a clear loser?
- How did I feel after I expressed my anger?
- Was my sense of justice restored?
- Did I feel closer to the other person or more distant?
- Did I feel more in control of my situation or more helpless?
- Did I feel guilty about my own aggressive behavior?
- Did I worry that the other person might retaliate?
- Did I feel resentful about giving in?
- Did the anger go away or did it linger?
- Did I feel healthier and happier or tense and irritable?

Systematic observation of the occasions, patterns, and results of expressing your anger will reveal a world of information you can use to prepare more effective alternative responses the next time.

Since the goal throughout this book is to gain insight into difficult behavior patterns and change them, neither rehearsing anger with friends, nor displacing anger by taking it out on inanimate objects or less powerful individuals, does anything to resolve the problem you have with the real target of your anger. It is advisable to note here that the direct expression of anger while you are still angry is seldom beneficial unless something changes for the better as a result. If your expression of anger results in a positive change in attitude and/or behavior on your part and that of the other person, if it clears the air, it is probably worth the effort and risk involved. If you can each walk away from an angry encounter with a sense of having reached a common ground, and without residual resentment or a desire to seek revenge, it was probably a good idea. However, it is seldom possible to predict these beneficial results in advance, and impossible to guarantee them, especially with your difficult customers. You simply cannot control what other people will choose to do.

Writing down your deepest thoughts and feelings does not directly resolve your emotionally painful issues with other people. On the other hand, however, it does lead to insights and understandings about your own needs, intentions, and attitudes, and to potentially constructive changes in your own behavior. Acknowledging your feelings to yourself in writing gives you the time and distance you need to face problems, work through them, and move beyond them at your own pace. If you can stop blaming others for your uncomfortable feelings, and stop inflicting your emotional rehearsals on your associates, you might be amazed at the positive change in their attitudes and your attractiveness to them. If you fail to choose the assertive response, if you fail to place the responsibility for this "self-work" into your own hands, you will probably continue to either (1) play the passive "victim," or (2) play the aggressive persecutor. Either role has short-term rewards, but in the long-run you alienate others and are always in danger of becoming overwhelmed by the fearful, shameful, guilty, or angry feelings you carry around with you and relive in your daily encounters with them.

Remember that everyone experiences anger sometimes. However, you do not have to be the passive victims of your own or anyone else's anger and abuse. Assertiveness is the key. You can take positive steps to deal with anger, including those outlined above. You can make a conscious commitment to seek out, focus on, and enjoy the positive rather than negative aspects of events and people's behavior, as difficult as they may be to find sometimes. You can remind yourself of positive experiences you have had in the past with people. You can take charge of your own thinking and substitute calming, reinforcing thoughts for negative or upsetting ones. You can apply humor to many angry situations. You can practice empathy, giving your difficult customer the benefit of the doubt, and the chance to save face as you try to understand his or her life or point of view. Instead of taking others' difficult behavior personally, you can opt for compassion without compromising assertiveness. You can decide for yourself if something is really worth being angry about and choose your own best alternative for resolving the issue.

As Mary might (assertively) say to Jane:

It really is upsetting for you to have to deal with a notice like that, especially when you're ready to drop after such a long trip. I'm so glad you brought this to my attention before the holiday weekend. It sounds like there's been a mistake somewhere. Let's sit down and see if we can figure out what to do about it!

You can learn to take care of yourself while dealing with others' difficult and angry behavior.

# 5 DEALING WITH ANGRY, AGGRESSIVE BEHAVIOR

People pack their emotional baggage every morning and take it with them wherever they go. Some people are capable of parking it in a corner of their mind somewhere while they are at work or out in public. But others cannot seem to resist opening it up upon arrival and making sure everyone knows what is in it.

Consider the following example:

> I'm so mad I can hardly see straight! What kind of witless person would let a nine-year-old check out an R-rated video from the library? Doesn't anybody use common sense anymore? I want to talk to the S.O.B. who's responsible for this—immediately! This is an outrage!

---

## OVERT AGGRESSION

There are a number of behaviors that identify the difficult customer as overtly aggressive (OA) when they occur frequently and chronically. This is the pattern of behavior that seems to trigger the most fear in library staff members. It is characterized by constant arguing, shouting, temper tantrums, sarcasm, and other tactics that allow the OA to ventilate openly his or her anger on a willing or unwilling convenient target. OAs engage in one-way communication, talking *at* rather than *with* others. They can be poor at listening but very practiced at giving orders, opinions, and unsolicited advice to others, often resulting in submission by the others. The sudden ferocity of an OA's outburst throws the listener off-balance into a state of temporary shock and confusion. When this happens, many people shift their response behavior to one extreme or the other and stay there. Depending upon how competent we are, and how confident we feel about our own abilities to handle it, OA behavior may induce us to respond to the OA's underlying needs and intentions in assertive, effective ways or to react in ineffective, unproductive ways, ranging from passive withdrawal to aggressive counterattack. If we normally feel in control and ready to meet challenges as they arise, we will probably have less difficulty handling confrontations with OAs than someone who feels generally helpless or powerless.

### UNDERSTANDING THE OVERTLY HOSTILE AND AGGRESSIVE PERSON

People who habitually express their anger in aggressive, competitive ways when frustrated or under stress are usually covering a powerful need to be in control of things and people. When they are *not* angry, they may simply display a highly task-focused, assertive, Type II persona.

Type IIs tend to be energetic, achievement-oriented people who can see what needs to be done and then proceed to do it the way *they* think it should be done. They like things to be in order and are uncomfortable with ambiguity and chaos. In their single-mindedness and directness, they can appear insensitive to other people's feelings and needs. They like to be in charge, make decisions, and direct others in what to do and how to do it. They are eager to finish one task and move on to the next one, often sacrificing precision for speed. *Many nondifficult people fall into this Type II category*. Some, however, have more difficulty handling their own frustration and anger than others do; when threatened or angry, they can become extremely competitive, hostile, and aggressive toward other people.[1] Some OAs manifest their aggressiveness right out in the open for all to see. Others prefer to take their shots from behind a protective screen of wit or sarcasm. Each of these manifestations will be explored in more detail in this chapter.

## The Overtly Aggressive Bully

Depending on the nature and frequency of their difficult behavior patterns, some overtly aggressive people might be classified as either part-time or full-time bullies. Like most other Type IIs, they want to get things done ASAP (*now*). They have a strong need to take control of most situations because they believe that being in charge will enable them to get things done and solve problems. Their *normal* communication with others tends to be straight to the point and action-oriented, rather than people-oriented.

However, because their emotional trigger is relatively sensitive, OAs can be unruffled one minute and explode the next. When they perceive that things are out of control, they can become upset to the point of running roughshod over the rights and feelings of other people, whom they accuse of creating the problem. (Witness Jane's outburst in the previous chapter.) Natural leaders, OAs often take risks and make spur-of-the-moment decisions on the basis of incomplete or inaccurate information. They then swing into action to implement those decisions, regardless of the objections of others who are more analytical, or who may have information that challenges the OAs' judgments. When other people do not share their vision, or if they fail to receive the credit they deserve for their accomplishments, OAs experience distress, and become impatient, then angry, viewing others not as persons but as obstacles in their path.

They may have learned in childhood that they could be more successful at getting what they wanted by throwing a temper tantrum than by asking for it. This behavior gets carried over into adulthood, where it is regularly reinforced by others' passive compliance. When frustrated or threatened, action-oriented OAs move into aggressive action, demanding obedience, yelling threats, and hurling insults. When in full force, they use "in-your-face" intimidation and arrogance to overpower their weaker adversaries and to win, no matter what.

Of course, the win-lose approach can never bring about a truly permanent victory. As long as the loser has some self-esteem left, he or she is likely to maintain resentment toward the winner until some way, peaceful or otherwise, can be found to restore balance to the scales of justice. If, by some chance, an OA loses the battle to an opponent who is stronger, he or she may either openly seek revenge on that person or go underground into passive-aggressiveness (to be discussed in the next chapter).

## STAND UP AND TAKE A STAND

An OA bully depends on a victim's passive acquiescence to attacks to achieve his or her goals. Therefore, to maximize the odds of a win-win solution, and to achieve your goal of establishing a common ground of mutual respect, you will have to move your response forward in a more assertive direction, while still underplaying the degree of aggressiveness your difficult customer is displaying. This means standing up to the OA and holding your ground until he or she can calm down and begin moving in your direction. Standing up to an OA, then, does not mean further polarizing the situation by defending yourself, fighting back, or arguing about who is right and who is wrong. These choices are a waste of time and energy. They are akin to pouring oil on a fire that is already raging out of control.

Once the momentum is under way, it is virtually impossible for OAs to give in or suddenly reverse direction. However, if you can keep them engaged in an interaction with you, they will eventually run out of the tremendous energy it takes to maintain their tantrum. You can begin standing up to an OA by literally standing up, if you are seated, and placing yourself and the OA in direct eye-contact. Standing up and holding your ground requires a conscious decision *ahead of time* that you intend to deal with such people assertively and not be knocked off-balance by their bluster, no matter how obnoxious they may appear.

One of the most effective steps in achieving this solid position is to look an OA squarely in the eyes while forcing yourself to breathe slowly and deeply. Both fear and anger (the ancient flight-or-fight response) are associated with lack of eye contact and quick, shallow breathing. By consciously practicing deep, regular breathing, you increase the flow of oxygen to the brain, which will help you to think more clearly and signal your body to relax, while you wait for the OA to run out of steam. Maintaining eye contact and holding your position by controlling both your emotions and your responses are examples of assertive behavior. If you have trouble getting and keeping an aggressor's attention, you can say his or her name loudly enough to be heard above the turmoil (e.g., "Jane," "Ms. Smith," or whatever you would normally use when addressing the person). You should keep repeating the person's name, along with phrases like, "Wait a minute!" or "I hear you!" until he or she begins to return eye contact.

When an OA sees you moving forward assertively, without threatening or surrendering, he or she may very well begin to back off and calm down. By firmly maintaining your non-aggressive, but assertive, position, you are helping the aggressor to regain self-control and save face. This in itself is a indication of your respect, the fact that you take him or her seriously, and that you wish to *cooperate* rather than to compete or antagonize. Assertively standing up to the OA and refusing to either retaliate or take abuse is also a way of communicating your *own* self-respect, and potentially winning the bully's respect as well. It tells potentially abusive OAs that, if they want your cooperation, they will have to behave in less intense, less aggressive, more assertive, and more mutually respectful ways themselves.

You can count on the OA to eventually run out of energy, grow tired, and calm down. He or she may even fall completely silent. This is your cue to suggest a break in the proceedings. Taking a walk, if possible, or moving to a more private location allows you and the OA time to regain lost composure. Once the OA has calmed down and is ready to talk (and perhaps even listen), it will be easier to apply the basic communication skills discussed in Chapter 2 (verbal and nonverbal reflection and exploration of the specifics of the problem or situation), and seek the person's cooperation in setting goals and solving the problems that are standing in the way of getting this person's needs met.

You should always try discover and keep in mind the underlying *needs and intentions* of the other person, regardless of their distracting and ineffective behaviors. OAs want to get things done. They also need recognition and appreciation for their accomplishments and their ideas about how to do things right. By stating the facts as you see them (using "I" statements), and offering your own opinions in the context of an OA's goals, you can move together toward a "win-win" solution that meets the needs of both of you. For example, you can show the difficult OA how additional fact-gathering and analysis, rather than *wasting time*, can actually help him or her achieve success and *save time* by avoiding unforseen obstacles. To the Type II, task-oriented person, this is forward-movement. At the same time, you will gain the satisfaction of having communicated assertively and having had your own ideas heard and respected. Ideally, the interaction will result in a gain in self-esteem for both of you. If you apply these assertive tactics consistently, the OA is less likely to resort to tantrum tactics in the future. Once you get to the heart of the OA's underlying needs for *control and appreciation*, and move with him or her in the direction of fulfilling those needs, the OA's behavior will often change very quickly from ranting and raving to quiet and calm.

It helps to remind yourself that you are probably not the real target of the person's anger at all but rather a safe object upon which he or she can displace anger. You may have inadvertently pushed one of the OA's hot buttons by saying certain words, using a certain tone of voice, presenting a facial expression, or doing something else that sets the person off. It is quite possible that, for some reason you may never know, the OA is angry at a spouse, boss, or someone else, but cannot safely express this anger for fear of negative repercussions. The fact that the OA trusts you enough to ventilate anger without fear of punishment, could (by a stretch of imagination) be interpreted as a kind of back-handed compliment. This idea is certainly not much consolation when *you* are under fire. However, if you can identify what the OA's emotional triggers are, you can often use this knowledge to determine what his or her underlying needs and intentions are, or at least take steps to avoid using the words or expressions that trigger or escalate his or her aggressive eruptions.

## WHO ASKED YOU?

One of the most annoying behaviors of OAs is their self-righteous habit of giving unsolicited advice. You can make extraordinary progress in your relationships with the OAs you work with, and command their respect at the same time, by *asking* them for feedback on your ideas and projects *before* they have a chance to initiate the advice themselves. At other times, when they interrupt something you are doing to tell you how to do it, politely but firmly let them know that you will accept feedback from them but only on *your* terms. To accomplish this in a way which allows you to finish what you were doing *your way*, and at the same time permits an OA to save face, you should present your statement as a "when-then" proposition. For example, you might say, "When I have finished working up these budget figures, I'd like you to look at them and comment." This communicates the message that you intend to finish what you are currently doing, and that when you finish, then (and *only* then) will you be interested in hearing his or her comments, if the person still wishes to do so. Asking OAs for feedback *when they are not being actively aggressive* is a way of giving them control, which is what they want to begin with. OAs handle others' passive *or* aggressive behavior with aggression. They are far more likely to respect and respond in kind to assertive behavior.

# COVERT AGGRESSION

Not every hostile person is capable of exercising the explosive intimidation tactics profiled above to express anger and resentment. There are some who, because of deeply ingrained social pressures or perceived powerlessness, cannot afford to explode and let the chips fall where they may. They take out their hostilities in much more subtle ways. Robert Bramson refers to these difficult customers as "snipers," the ones who take potshots at us from behind a protective cover of social-acceptance, often thinly disguising their volleys in the form of sarcasm, jokes, innuendos, stage whispers, teasing, or witticisms that are actually intended to hurt the other person.[2] The behavior of these covert aggressives (CAs) is a step above the kind of passive-aggressive behavior described in the next chapter, in that it is at least partially *conscious and verbal*. However, this conniving CA behavior can be just as disconcerting as the more unconscious, non-verbal passive-aggressive behavior or the blatant OA pattern. The recipient in all three cases is thrown off balance about what to do. For example, suppose Mary's encounter with the outraged Jane had gone something like this instead:

> Jane enters the branch public library one Friday afternoon at about 5:20 p.m., and walks calmly to the circulation desk.

There are two staff members on duty at the desk, one of whom, Mike, is charging out materials to a middle-aged woman and her five-year-old grandson. The other staff member, Mary, is busy tidying up the work area before the library closes at 5:30 for the weekend. Monday is a holiday, the library will be closed until Tuesday morning, and Mary is looking forward to the extra day off and a chance to catch up with her garden and her own grandchildren. Jane approaches Mary, smiles at everyone, and announces for all to hear: "I just got home from a week-long business trip, and I'm sitting down to relax and go through the mail, when the first thing I see is this 'bill' for an overdue book. Tell me," she says, smiling all the while, "isn't the library an odd place for people of marginal literacy and intelligence to be working?" As the five-year-old squirms and the grandmother and Mike nervously smile at Jane's clever little insult, Mary tries to hide her hurt and embarrassment behind a forced smile, and hopes that her supervisor hasn't overheard Jane's remark, too.

Paradoxically, the *cover* that protects CAs is usually provided by the victims who don't want to call negative attention to themselves, create further unpleasantness, or admit that anything adverse is taking place. The target of a CA's witty barbs will often laugh along with the rest of the crowd, pretending to be a good sport in order to avoid a direct confrontation, all the while fuming inside with helpless resentment. Behind this social cover, the CA is protected from any retaliation that might occur if the attack were more open and direct.

Many victims of CAs find it very difficult to deal with them assertively when other people are around. More often than not, witnesses to these verbal potshots also feel angry and uncomfortable and secretly long for the victim to strike back. However, they refrain from speaking up for fear of becoming targets themselves.

Like armed snipers, CAs wait behind their social covers for the moment when their target is most vulnerable before taking their shots. The resulting injury to the victim's self-esteem and personal power gives the CA the sense of control that he or she desperately needs.

While this process is taking place, real problems often go unidentified, unexplored, and unsolved. A CA's difficult behavior pattern can bring some of the most action-oriented leaders or groups to a complete halt. Without the opportunity for a fair fight, individuals and groups can become discouraged, even demoralized. Eventually people's productivity and commitment to service suffer as a result.

## Why do CAs act that way?

Like OAs, they often have very fixed ideas about what needs to be done and how to do it. This outlook leads them to see others as potential adversaries with whom they must compete to get their needs met and goals accomplished. Neither OAs nor CAs tolerate losing gracefully. Their extremely aggressive, competitive styles make it hard for them to understand, even listen, to others' points of view. As a result, their communication tends to be one-way (*their* way). In addition, like OAs, CAs frequently set unreasonably high standards for their own and others' behavior. The primary difference between OAs and CAs is the way they choose to enforce these standards. CAs tend to be much more self-conscious and resourceful than OAs. For CAs, behaving in an openly aggressive or abusive way would mean they were out of control, which would be intolerable. When others fail to meet their unrealistic expectations, they resort instead to sarcasm, cutting remarks, or other indirect verbal assaults to punish or coerce their victims into doing what the CAs think they should do.

A particularly vicious variation of CA-type behavior, widely reported in libraries and other nonprofit agencies, is the practice of putting the self-righteous or insulting comments in *writing*. The note or memo is sent to the target to be read later, after the sender has gone or is otherwise inaccessible. Anecdotal accounts of this practice often involve an employer who perceives the employee as a threat to his or her sense of control, either because the employee possesses some special knowledge or skill, or simply because the employee is perceived as different in some way. (In the latter case, the employee may become a convenient scapegoat for the supervisor's covert hostility against the employee's racial, gender, religious, or ethnic group.) Instead of using the opportunities available for face-to-face conversations about what is bothering him or her, the CA supervisor makes sure that the receiver reads the upsetting memo under circumstances that make an immediate response impossible (for example, when the sender is "busy," in a meeting, or gone for the day).

Since the sender has virtually removed any opportunity for direct two-way communication, the receiver must bear the burden for initiating a response alone. Such hit-and-run behavior on the part of a supervisor can leave an employee feeling shaken, worried and defenseless, wondering how or even whether to respond at all. The sender takes advantage of the receiver's inability to reply immediately to escape the consequences of the act, and uses his or her inaccessibility as a effective hiding place. Complicating the situation is the high probability that the sender, again wishing to avoid direct confrontation, will not even mention the memo again. Indeed, the CA memo writer is depending on the receiver *not* to respond.

Rather than risk engaging in, and possibly losing, an open conflict with people they view as in control (and, therefore, more powerful), CAs concentrate on undercutting their opponents, striking where and when their enemy is weakest and most vulnerable. This results in a restoration (at least in the CAs' minds) of the balance of power, without injury to the CAs.

From their position of perceived powerlessness, CAs often exaggerate the actual power of others in their own minds. For example, they may expect others in more powerful positions to be able to make immediate changes in policies when, in fact, they may *not* be able to do so.

CAs hone their sniping skills over time, receiving reinforcement for their sharpshooting in the laughter and reluctant admiration of others, and in the absence of immediate negative consequences. While OAs paint their aggressive picture out in the open with broad brush strokes, CAs employ precision instruments with pinpoint accuracy while enjoying relative protection from exposure.

### Exposing the Covert Aggressive's Camouflage

If forced to choose between dealing with an OA or a CA, anyone who has ever been the victim of a covertly aggressive person's skillful sabotage would probably choose the honest pounding of the OA's misguided abuse over being skewered by the CA's poisonous verbal arrows. However, the relative powerlessness of CAs, which forces them into hiding, is also the key to dealing more effectively with them. As long as they can maintain their protective social cover, they are virtually invulnerable. Therefore, when dealing with this type of difficult customer, it is essential to remove that cover. The easiest way to do this is to wait until you are alone with the CA (or arrange a private moment), and say something like, "Jane, when you made that funny remark about people of marginal intelligence and literacy working at the library, I thought I heard an insult in that. Did you mean it that way?" Jane then may choose either to switch to open aggression ("Yes, I did. Only someone who can't read simple book titles, names, and addresses could have made a stupid mistake like that. . . ."), or to deny that the remark was a camouflaged attack ("Of course not, Mary. Can't you take a joke? I've always been impressed with the library staff's knowledge and intelligence"). If the CA switches to open hostility and aggression, you should use the techniques recommended earlier in this chapter for dealing with overt aggresives.

Another strategy, designed to remove the protective cover that hides a CA's real purpose in making a remark, is to pause, look the person right in the eyes, and say "Jane, I just heard you say it was odd for people of marginal intelligence and literacy to be working in a library. When you say we are marginally intelligent and literate, what are you *really* trying to say?" You may have to repeat this sequence of reflecting several times to get to the underlying needs or intention.

If a CA's chronic attempts to get attention and appear witty are keeping you and your associates from moving ahead on a project or solving a problem, the way to get the real intentions and needs out of hiding is to use verbal and nonverbal reflection, then ask, for example, "Bob, I thought we were meeting here to start working on a new personnel policy manual. How does . . . (restate whatever the CA has just said) help us to get started?" Again, persistence and repetition are required.

When others are watching, it is much easier for a CA to hide behind the protective social context and deny the ulterior intent of the "joke." However, regardless of the degree of privacy you are able to provide, removing the CA's cover is essential to stopping this difficult behavior pattern. Remember: The CA's characteristic pattern of difficult behavior has been developed and reinforced over a long period of time. It is not likely to change as the result of one or even several attempts on your part to "smoke them out." However, if you are able, through your own assertive behavior, to get the CA to level with you, by all means you should use your basic communication skills to help them express their feelings and goals in a non-aggressive, non-defensive manner. This process will help you achieve a common ground with them and will set the stage for more direct, cooperative behavior in the future.

You should be prepared to be friendly but you shouldn't fail to behave assertively! You need to let both OAs and CAs know that it is safe for them to talk to you in confidence about things that make them angry, reinforcing their efforts to be honest and straightforward by *not* resorting to aggressive behavior yourself.

# References

1. See *The Library Survival Guide: Managing the Problem Situation*, a 20-minute videocassette tape (Chicago: American Library Association/Library Video Network, 1987)

    Please note that the type of aggression described in this chapter refers *only* to anger-driven behavior that is *verbal* in nature. In no way is the author suggesting that anyone attempt to apply the suggested responses when there is a clear threat of physical violence and injury. When physical danger is a reality, it is imperative that we do whatever we can to escape or prevent harm to ourselves and others.

    Library staff members should know and be able to take appropriate steps to ensure their own security and safety and that of others in the library. Training in these procedures is strongly recommended for all library staff. The tape details several problem situations in the library and how to respond to them. It presents dramatic illustrations of disruptive situations, including threatening and non-threatening behaviors, and can be used as a starting point for training and staff discussion.
2. Robert M. Bramson, *Coping with Difficult People*. (New York: Ballantine Books, 1981), 22-23.

# 6 DEALING WITH PASSIVE-AGGRESSIVE BEHAVIOR

What? You have a five-page database search, 15 photocopies, and 17 interlibrary loan books for me on nuclear lump theory? But I've decided to switch my research focus and do the paper on another topic. I guess I forgot to tell you. Thanks, anyway. Just send the books back.

In our society, we find evidence of a strange, but increasingly common, paradox: *passive-aggressive behavior*. To live in society with others we all have to tame our aggressive tendencies to some extent to conform with laws and cultural expectations. Habitually passive-aggressive persons (PAs), however, seem to be engaged in a continual, but largely unconscious, psychic struggle between (1) their own *hostile tendencies* and (2) highly rigid, internalized *cultural prohibitions* against the open expression of conflict with others. Passive-aggression differs from other types of covert aggression in that it can be much more difficult to identify and handle. For example, with a covertly aggressive sniper (CA), the aggression is at least verbal and intentional. With a PA, the agenda is hidden from *both* parties.

## THE PASSIVE-AGGRESSIVE PERSON

The PA will often pursue hurtful and confusing motives, under the guise of friendship and caring, but inflicting pain and destruction in a way that leaves the recipient disarmed and confused. The passive-aggressor is likely to be unconscious of his or her competitive motivation to win or exert control over others. In fact, PAs will probably *deny* any such self-motivation if confronted with the idea by others. Acknowledgment of any hostile or aggressive intent on their part would be incongruent with their view of themselves as nice, well-meaning people. Unlike the sniping engaged in by covert hostile-aggressives (CAs), the PA's behavior is much more challenging and frustrating to deal with because their motivations are as much or more hidden from *themselves* as from the others who become their victims. At least with CAs, one can draw the sniper out of the safety of his or her hiding place. The rigid psychological defense mechanisms of PAs deny the existence of a hideout altogether.

**69**

PAs are among the most difficult of the difficult customers we encounter in the library. Likewise, supervisors who are PAs can be especially burdensome. Consider the following illustration:

### Debra

Debra has a reputation among her peers outside the library as a professional who has risen through the ranks to become director of one of her region's larger libraries by being an intelligent, effective administrator. She comes across as a thoughtful, though somewhat colorless and passive, *nice* person. The child of a military officer, Debra lived in many different places while growing up. Her entire library career, however, has been in the institution where she is now the director. While a graduate student, Debra started working as a paraprofessional assistant in the reference department. There, because of her pleasant and deferring demeanor, she won the attention of the library director, a "benevolent dictator," who became her mentor. Upon receipt of her library science degree, Debra was appointed to a reference librarian position. Over the next few years, she was promoted first to reference department head, then to assistant director, as these positions became vacant. Debra served as assistant director for seven years, faithfully supporting and carrying out the decisions of her mentor, the director. She discovered early on that unquestioning support for the director's authority and quiet compliance with his dictates were rewarded, whereas constructive suggestions and other forms of risk-taking and innovation were gently but clearly discouraged.

Debra's ambition was to step into the director job upon her mentor's retirement, and she was confident that she was next in line. In order to survive while she bided her time, she managed to keep any creative and innovative impulses under wraps, and as the years went by, this became easier and easier. Debra knew instinctively that, with her quiet nonconfrontative persona, she could not duplicate the director's authoritarian style.

When her mentor retired, she was appointed director on his recommendation. She was determined to introduce what she believed would be a more participative style of management into the library.

Debra began holding regular monthly staff meetings with her middle managers and first-line supervisors, during which everyone exchanged information on current activities in their departments. From time to time, after announcing her latest decisions and directives, Debra invited the members of the group to comment and offer suggestions for improvement and change. After so many years of the previous director's kindly dictatorship, this move on

Debra's part was a welcome relief to the more creative, achievement-oriented members of her staff. A few of the more courageous staff members saw this as an opportunity to air thoughts and feelings, both positive and negative, that they had had for a long time.

One of the more assertive department heads, Jocelyn, took the initiative of presenting her ideas for improving service, policies, and procedures to the director in writing, with a request that they be discussed at a future staff meeting. Jocelyn had recently joined the library staff as head of public services. She had been told by Debra in her interview that the library needed "new blood," managers who could identify areas that needed changing, and who could provide the necessary leadership and follow-through. However, Jocelyn heard nothing from Debra about her memo. The two happened to meet in the hallway a few days prior to a staff meeting, so Jocelyn casually asked Debra if she had any comments on her proposal. Debra politely replied that she had not had the time to read everything completely but would do so as soon as she could. Jocelyn assumed that her carefully reasoned proposal would eventually receive the full consideration of the director, and would also be discussed, if not at the next meeting, in the near future.

Despite regular follow-ups from Jocelyn, three months passed with no response from Debra other than, "Oh, yes, I intend to get back to that, but we have so many other, more pressing problems to worry about. Well, . . . you know how it is. As soon as we get some breathing room, maybe we'll have the leisure to talk about some new ideas." At each staff meeting, Debra continued her practice of asking the group for comments and suggestions on her predetermined decisions and plans and received little or no response. Jocelyn, wary but still willing to trust Debra's good intentions, used the opportunity at one of these meetings to bring up one of the ideas she had previously submitted to Debra. In reply, Debra said, "Well, you know, we thought about doing that several years ago, before you were here, but we realized that it would be impossible." Debra then politely pointed out all the reasons why the idea would not work, either then or now, *except* for the real reason: The previous director, for reasons known only to himself, had refused to consider it, and Debra had been powerless to do anything except politely defer to his objections and stay in his good graces. Her need to comply with the *status quo* outweighed her desire to be more democratic.

Jocelyn came away from the meeting feeling confused, chastened, and betrayed. Still giving Debra the benefit of the doubt about her participatory intentions, she tried a few more times to initiate constructive change. Debra continued to set up roadblocks to new input from Jocelyn and other staff (for their own good), all under the guise of *caring* about them and *helping* them avoid the certain failure of their proposed ideas. Jocelyn, determined to maintain her own sanity, finally gave up the struggle. She found a new position elsewhere.

This unfortunate scenario illustrates the kind of emotionally draining effect PAs can have on others. Debra managed to maintain her nice persona (caring, friendly, participatory-minded) by feigning powerlessness (to implement Jocelyn's proposed changes) and using it to totally control Jocelyn and the other members of her staff.

### HOW DID THE PASSIVE-AGGRESSIVE GET THAT WAY?

PAs typically have problems in relating to authority figures that they resolve by deferring to that authority. Quite often, they come from authoritarian home environments in which the expression of negative emotions, especially anger, was forbidden. Eventually, they learned to repress these aggressive feelings and impulses, for the most part. This denial or lack of awareness about their aggressive tendencies is what makes and keeps PAs so invulnerable to change.

### RECOGNIZING PASSIVE-AGGRESSIVE BEHAVIOR

To offset their unwillingness or inability to acknowledge and express these forbidden feelings directly, PAs develop a number of behaviors, each carefully designed to further their ulterior motive of gaining power and control over others. They accomplish this by indirectly and unconsciously inflicting psychological injury.

PA behaviors vary in appearance and impact. They range from procrastination and tardiness to forgetfulness and chronic misunderstanding, to game-playing. These behaviors are difficult to diagnose accurately because they are practiced by just about everyone from time to time, so the ulterior motives behind them are largely invisible. If the PA engages in one of these forms of behavior, he or she may very well be unconsciously using it to express some resentment or hostility while avoiding the internal and external consequences of direct confrontation.

Let's look more closely at the forms of passive-aggressive behavior:

**Procrastination:** This behavior is characterized by numerous needless delays, resulting in the *victim* becoming annoyed and distressed. The PA may further compound the injury by labeling the victim as irritable, impatient, or "too intense" or using other shame-inducing ploys. We all procrastinate or miss deadlines occasionally. However, for the PA, procrastination functions as a weapon, to be used in specific situations against specific individuals. It is a highly effective way for PAs to exercise control over another person while maintaining the pretense of innocence.

**Tardiness:** As with procrastination, PAs seem to target their lateness to specific situations and individuals. For example, they may be chronically late for work or for regularly scheduled meetings while offering a variety of marginally believable excuses. ("Can you believe it? It's the second flat tire I've had this week!")

**Forgetfulness:** From time to time, we all forget things we intended to remember, especially if we are distracted by other events or if we fail to write them down. However, with the PA, forgetting is consistent and seems specifically targeted toward certain persons, not everyone. The PA, for example, will chronically *forget* to do things that he or she has consented to do for *that* person. Rather than take the risk of directly refusing a request, especially one from an authority figure, or of stating that he or she does not really *want* to do it, the PA will politely agree, then not deliver. Forgetting, along with procrastination, is a behavior often exhibited by yes-people (to be described in a later chapter). However, while the yes-person's basic intent is to maintain a good working relationship, the passive-aggressor's intent is to manipulate and control with impunity.

**Chronic Misunderstanding and Refusal to Learn:** Understanding is one of the major goals of interpersonal communication. Anyone who makes a commitment to reaching a common ground of understanding with another will consistently apply the principles of good communication, such as active listening and clarification, to overcome perceived differences, conflict, and misunderstandings. However, for a PA, misunderstandings can function as another weapon to *get* someone. For example, the PA might take disturbing information that we reported to him or her in confidence and relay it inaccurately to someone else so that person becomes extremely distressed and upset. The PA will then apologize profusely, saying, "I could have sworn you said Harry needed to be made aware of this problem!'' The PA's ''innocence'' remains intact, while our relationship with Harry is on the point of collapse. Or the PA will repeatedly and thoughtlessly wear a powerful brand of cologne in our presence, after we have informed her (or him) repeatedly that we usually have an allergic reaction to it. Upon being so informed (again), the PA will say something like, ''Gosh, I only used a couple of drops!'' or ''I thought you were taking medication for that!''

**Game-Playing:** Eric Berne, the founder of Transactional Analysis, defined ''games'' as ''sets of ulterior transactions, repetitive in nature, with a well-defined psychological payoff.''[1] Games are characterized by indirect behavior and ulterior motives. The game-player appears to be engaging in friendly, innocuous conversation with another while he or she is actually subverting the relationship. He or she plays on some weakness of the opponent, such as fear, greed, annoyance, or emotional attachment, and hooks the opponent into playing out the transaction. The game-player then turns the tables on the opponent by pulling some sort of trick or switch, leaving the opponent confused and vulnerable. The payoff, which is usually emotional in nature, then follows for both parties.

# PLAYING GAMES

Passive-aggressive people are often experts at this type of game-playing, which they habitually offer as an alternative to direct communication. Instead of building relationships, game-players sabotage them. Five of the more common games played by PAs are outlined below. All are designed to give PAs (who unconsciously perceive themselves as powerless and out of control) an illusion of power and control.

1. *''I'm in Charge.''* The purpose of this power-play game is to maintain the PA's feeling of superior power or position in the face of others whom he or she perceives as a threat (which can include just about everyone, regardless of intent to threaten). Examples of typical tactics include a

PA taking credit and recognition without sharing it with those who have done the work; obstructing coworkers' or subordinates' progress simply because he or she is in a position to do so; and delaying the progress of a group by constantly directing the group's attention to himself or herself. For example, a committee is working to develop a new policy statement. The members are making great progress in spite of the fact that one of them, a game-player, has attended fewer than half of the committee's meetings (presumably due to more urgent and important matters). After each meeting, the committee chair sends everyone, including the absent members, minutes of the meeting and copies of the latest drafts of the policy in order to confirm what has been discussed and decided. Rather than communicate directly with the chair or others outside of the meetings for an update, the game-player (when there) repeatedly interrupts the current group meeting to debate the meaning of a word or to *suggest* alternative wording (which the group had discussed thoroughly and rejected two meetings ago!). The game-player has *hooked* the others' desire to be democratic and informative, to include everyone in the discussion. By keeping them diverted from their current business until time runs out, the PA manages to achieve the desired power-and-control payoff. Other members of the group, including the chair, do not realize they have been conned until the time allowed for the meeting has expired and they experience their own payoff—frustration at having met without making further progress. Unless someone realizes that a power-and-control game has transpired, that all have been duped, and who the perpetrator actually is, the irritation may be directed at the chair for not keeping the meeting focused on the agenda.

2. *"Why Don't You (We)."* This game is commonly played by Would-Be Know-It-Alls (WBKIAs) (*see* Chapter 10), some of whom are also passive-aggressive. The game-player offers *helpful* information and recommendations, whether asked for or not. Victims get conned into believing that the perpetrator's advice is valid only to discover they have been had. This game is often, but not always, followed by "You Fool." Victims often counteract this game with their own game of "Yes, But. . . ."

3. *"You Fool."* Sometimes referred to as "Gotcha"[2] or "Now I've Got You, You S.O.B." (NIGYSOB)[3], this game is

similar to "I'm in Charge" in that the perpetrator's payoff is the illusion of power. This game is especially attractive to the PA who has a weak sense of personal power. The characteristic behaviors include setting others up for failure by hooking them into making errors, delaying their progress so they miss deadlines, and other sabotage. The payoff bolsters the perpetrator's fragile ego, which manifests itself externally in some form of "I told you so" or in internal exultation at the victim's inadequacies.

4. *"Pit Bull."* This game appears in several varieties, depending on who participates. People who play it scream and shout at each other to no useful purpose. The payoff is the ventilation of hostility, not the healthy expression of anger. The result is that everyone's attention is sidetracked from the business at hand to the game-players themselves. Sometimes this game involves *more* than two persons, with the winner the one who can shout the longest and loudest, while the losers share a feeling of resentment. In a more subtle version of this game, the perpetrator refrains from direct participation in the fight but sets up a situation in which others turn on each other. One way of doing this is to innocently pass information along to person A about something person B has said or done that the game-player knows person A is sensitive about. Person A then goes off to settle the score with person B while the game-player exults in his or her power to manipulate. Needless to say, nothing productive occurs while time is being used for the fight and its aftermath.

5. *"Alas."* This is another game that feeds into the PA's experience of powerlessness and corresponding need to gain power and control. In it, the person who is perceived as more powerful gets to play "Why Don't You (We)" while the "Alas" player responds with all the reasons why the advice won't work. The payoff of this "Yes, But . . ." tactic is, again, diversion of attention to the game-players rather than solution to a problem or the strengthening of a relationship.

The player of "Alas," like the chronic complainers described in Chapter 7, may do nothing to correct or eliminate the cause of the complaint. However, unlike the garden variety complainer, the passive-aggressive "Alas" player is not particularly well-meaning. Rather, he or she gets reinforcement for the game-playing behavior from the illusory feelings of power resulting from the game.

It is extremely difficult to deal with passive-aggressive game-players without cutting off communication altogether to avoid getting hooked into their game.

# WHAT TO DO?

To overcome the PA's habitual *misunderstanding* behavior, you should ask him or her to repeat back what you have said—or to put his or her understanding in writing.

To deal with the PA's habit of procrastination, you need to establish exact deadlines and clearly state what the consequences/penalties will be if those deadlines are not met. You should put these in writing (so that the PA cannot conveniently forget), and enforce the penalties.

The same strategy can be used to deal with habitual tardiness. For example, if a PA is always late for meetings, you should announce clearly (again, writing it down makes it more *real*) that all meetings will begin and end on time, and that no information will be repeated for those who are late. If a PA always keeps you waiting for scheduled appointments, you can tell him or her that you will wait ten minutes (or whatever waiting time is acceptable to you), but if he or she does not appear by then, you will leave. Of course, you must be willing to *enforce* the consequences you have stated.

George R. Bach and Herb Goldberg, in their book *Creative Aggression*,[4] offer a number of suggestions for dealing with all types of aggressiveness in other people, including chronic passive-aggressors. They strongly suggest self-examination as a starting point for understanding the interpersonal dynamics between a PA and his or her victim, including the following questions:

1. Am *I* overly controlling or dominating with this person and, therefore, making it impossible for the person to assert himself or herself more directly?
2. Am *I* actually more comfortable with passive-aggression and, even though it is frustrating and annoying, would I rather have that than have this person express his (or her) feelings openly to me?[5]

If you can honestly answer "no" to both questions, and if you sincerely wish to try a new approach, you have to be willing to:

1. Confront and acknowledge your own feelings of anger and/or guilt in these interactions;
2. Express your feelings about the other's behavior; and
3. Attempt to expose the hidden hostility underlying the PA's behavior so that you can talk about it and understand it.

## DON'T PLAY

An obvious method of dealing with passive-aggressive game-playing and other such tactics is to recognize the game for what it is and refuse to play. Remember that, regardless of the difficulty their behavior might pose to others, people are *always* trying to meet their own needs and goals. Those needs and goals have strong feelings and values attached to them. They may be so deeply concealed under defensive and contradictory behavior that the individuals may not even be aware that these feelings are there. Negative experiences in a person's formative years may have resulted in these feelings, needs, and goals going underground, forcing him or her to assume a cover that denies their existence but that does not make them go away. If you decide that it is worth your time and effort to try to effect change, and if you persevere in trying to identify what people's real feelings, needs, and goals are, you may be able to use this knowledge to get them to change their behavior toward you.

But also remember that long-term change requires that an individual have some degree of insight into his or her own feelings and motivations. He or she must desire and *choose* change in order for it to be effective and long-lasting. Such insight and desire may be lacking in the difficult person, especially if that person is a *successful* passive-aggressive. Therefore, it is probably more rational to keep expectations of change in the other person low and, instead, concentrate on changing your *own* behavior. This means persuading or acting as a *catalyst*.

Once you recognize the symptoms of passive-aggressiveness, particularly game-playing, you have to be vigilant about not getting hooked into the game. However, a direct approach—observing out loud that the other person is trying to play a game with you—will probably be met with denial and further defensiveness on the part of the PA.

If the passive-aggressive person happens to be your boss or someone else in a position of relatively higher authority, you may have tried active listening and other tactics described in this book in an effort to understand and establish a common (non-game-playing) ground. If these efforts have failed repeatedly, your best strategy may be to remind yourself of an important truth: *Healthy people seek healthy environments; unhealthy people tend to drag others down to their level.* For your own sanity's sake, there may come a time when you need to either leave the PA-dominated unhealthy environment entirely or to find mutual support through your more healthy associates and more direct and satisfying associations with people outside of the work environment.

No one *has* to be a victim! But you must realize that there are many things in life that are beyond your control. The story of Jim, Jack, and George may serve to illustrate:

> Jim is the pilot of a small private aircraft. Jack is the name he has given to his automatic pilot mechanism, the "black box" that keeps the plane on course to its destination. Jim picks his own destination. His black box (Jack) is in charge of the flight. It is Jack, the automatic pilot, who gets Jim to where he wants to go by a certain time. It is Jack who constantly checks with George, the instrument panel, who knows where the plane is now, and who can correct the course as needed.

Like Jim, you must envision and decide what your destination is. Then you look at where you are and decide when it might be reasonable to arrive there (in terms of how long it might take, given current conditions). Then you set a course to get there.

Any experienced pilot knows, however, that even with the best automatic pilot, *you are off course at least 90 percent of the time*! Jack knows what the course is. He can tell, by checking with George, how much the plane is deviating from that, and he instructs the plane's various mechanisms to correct the deviation so that you are back on course again, at least enough to get you where you want to be at approximately the time you want to be there (barring sudden prohibitive changes in the weather). But *you* decide. It is *your* black box and *your* instrument panel, not someone else's. Once you know the course settings, you can check your instruments (your own feelings, needs, and goals) often enough to make mid-course corrections as needed. But you must decide for yourself what you want, and give others the respect of being responsible for their own feelings and reactions, regardless of their ability or willingness to return that respect or assume that responsibility for themselves.

# References

1. Eric Berne, *What Do You Say After You Say Hello?* (New York: Bantam Books, 1973), 23.
2. Donald H. Weiss, *How to Deal with Difficult People.* (New York: American Management Association, 1987), 11.
3. Eric Berne, *Games People Play.* (New York: Grove Press, 1964), passim.
4. George R. Bach and Herb Goldberg. *Creative Aggression.* (Garden City, NY: Doubleday, 1974), passim.
5. Ibid., 47.

# 7 DEALING WITH COMPLAINERS

Who's in charge of buying books for children? I found these comic books in my son's book bag. He said he got them at the library. Is this how you people are spending the taxpayers' money these days?

I hate how Diane talks to our male patrons. She just isn't professional. You would think she would know better than to risk telling those double-entendre jokes the way she does. Why doesn't somebody tell her how she's ruining the library's reputation?

This chapter will examine a phenomenon commonly experienced by library staff—especially people who work in the public service areas of the library—the person who complains. Complaints and complainers come in many forms and contexts. They come from patrons, bosses, co-workers, subordinates, friends, family, and total strangers. We *all* reserve the right to complain from time to time. Indeed, the right to complain is an aspect of our right to freedom of speech, guaranteed by the Constitution. Some complainers, however, are easier to deal with than others and, depending on our individual skills and interpersonal styles, we may feel more comfortable and be more successful in handling the complaints of people we *don't* know than the complaints of those whom we *do* know. Likewise, a complainer may simply behave in an assertive way to get a problem resolved, *or* he or she may become a difficult customer—the chronic complainer.

## COMPLAINTS AND SERVICE

The effective handling of customer complaints is part of effective library service, part of the reason libraries exist. Every time a library staff member interacts with one of the library's patrons, he or she has an opportunity to provide either poor service, mediocre service, or first-class service. The interaction is also an opportunity to set the tone for all future contact between that person and the library. One incident of poor service can obliterate all memories of good treatment in the past. Likewise, one incident of friendly, effective service can undo many prior bad experiences a person has had with libraries. If quality service, including the effective handling of complaints, is not given emphasis in staff training, if library staff members are unaware of how important it is to treat customers well, and if they are indifferent to their opportunities to provide excellent service, the library's service (and perceived image) will become mediocre at best. If the staff continually handles complaints as if they were personal attacks, rather than as problems to be solved in a professional manner, both the image of the library and the quality of service will continue to deteriorate.

Complaints do not have to be followed by negative outcomes, for either the complainer or the library. When given and received as constructive criticism, complaints can help bring about awareness of needed changes, which can not only improve the complainer's situation but also have a positive effect on library policies *and* relationships in general. However, when a complaint is given ineffectively or received defensively, or when complaining is the habitual communication style of a particular person, it is more likely to keep people apart and prevent mutual problem-solving.

## COMPLAINTS ABOUT LIBRARY POLICIES, RULES, AND MISTAKES

Whether they are co-workers, patrons, family members, or personal friends and acquaintances, and regardless of their skill at communicating, be cautioned that people can and often do have *legitimate complaints*. Not all complainers are difficult customers. No one can afford to routinely construe all complainers as crackpots or worse, to take the defensive or even counterattack. When faced with a complaint, regardless of the content, *the goal is not to assign blame but to help the complainer to clarify and to solve the problem*. This sometimes means first acknowledging the existence of a problem that cannot be solved without the library's involvement and agreeing that a solution might require some change in library policy or procedure.

### Nancy

Suppose that a library's circulation policy says that new books may circulate for two weeks and may not be renewed so long as there are other people on the waiting list for them. Let's suppose that Nancy, for whom reading is a major form of relaxation and recreation, works full time and has only limited hours to devote to reading. Nancy has generally been able to finish reading the average best-seller within the two-week circulation period. However, the latest one she has been working on is an 850-page epic (for which she has already waited three months to read). She has only been able to get through the first 500 or so pages by the date it is due.

Other people are on the waiting list for the title, so Nancy's options are somewhat limited by library policy and procedure. Either she can return the book on time and put her name at the end of the waiting list to finish it several months down the road, or she can purposely keep it a week or more overdue, finish reading it, somewhat guiltily return it, and somewhat resentfully pay the overdue fine. Nancy has exercised each of these options on occasion in the past without complaint. A third option, buying her own copy to finish reading it, is too expensive for Nancy (especially since she has read over half the book already) and counterproductive for the library since it may lose Nancy as a satisfied, repeat patron, the backbone of any public service organization.

Whichever option Nancy chooses, she and the library both stand to lose. Therefore, she decides to register a complaint with the circulation person on duty, whom she does not know personally. If the library person she complains to reacts defensively, quoting policy again, and offers no other options for resolution of the problem, Nancy gets no satisfaction in the short term. Once burned by inflexible implementation of a policy, Nancy will be sensitized. She may misinterpret the library's policies as antagonistic even when they are not. If Nancy routinely and repeatedly experiences the library as a impersonal source of stress and conflict, the long-term cumulative effect is likely to be erosion of her goodwill toward the library or even avoidance.

Nancy is representative of the many responsible, reasonable patrons of libraries who find themselves at odds with inflexible policies. She reasons: How many people these days have the leisure or the single-mindedness to plow through an 800-plus-page book in two weeks, and still maintain a healthy balance among the other demands for their time and attention? Assuming that Nancy is justified in complaining about the library's circulation policy on new books being applied in this case, her complaint, if taken seriously, might result both in the resolution of her problem and in a more reasonable and flexible policy. Such a solution would benefit both patrons and the library in the future, in terms of high standards of service and goodwill toward the library.

## COMPLAINTS ABOUT LIBRARY MATERIALS

By stretching the imagination, one can view library policy and its enforcement as a way of communicating organizational intent, then see an analogy between *library* policies and procedures and *individual* communication process and content. Nancy's complaint dealt with a concrete procedure, the library's application of its circulation policy in the unusual case of an 800-page novel, as opposed to the content of the policy, which she acknowledged was the library's prerogative to determine.

Complaints about library materials, on the other hand, have to do with *content*, about which people certainly can disagree, and about which the library staff must use professional judgment. The methods libraries use to determine the content of the library's collection are covered well in other sources. How the library staff can best handle these content complaints, like any other complaints, is an interpersonal process, which will be discussed later in this chapter.

Suffice it to say that, for our purposes here, every library needs to have a sound policy on materials selection and collection development. This policy should allow for a reasonable and flexible set of procedures for dealing with complaints about materials, procedures that every staff member needs to understand and be able to apply when necessary. Beyond these organizationally prescribed methods, the most effective individual behaviors one can use to handle complaints are virtually the same regardless of the cause that prompts the complaint—whether the complaint is a one-time occurrence involving a stranger or comes from someone the library staff member knows to be a chronic complainer.

# DEALING WITH COMPLAINTS

First, you need to remember that gathering the courage to complain is difficult for many library users, particularly those who do not ordinarily complain about anything. Nancy, who complained about the library's circulation policy, is *not* a chronic complainer. She simply has asserted an objection. To handle objections, library staff members can gain control of such situations by taking the following recommended steps:

1. *Listen and acknowledge the objection.* If library staff are unclear about the content of the objection, they should ask the customer to explain. They should empathize by acknowledging a customer's feelings: "I can see that you are upset about this." They should listen *completely* before

trying to answer, giving the person undivided attention. They shouldn't interrupt. They should control their emotions by ignoring sarcasm and exaggeration. They shouldn't argue or try to place blame on the customer or some other department of the library. They can apologize for the customer's inconvenience, not accept *personal* responsibility for the problem.

2. *Deal with the objection immediately.* You need to take complaints seriously. You should not ignore them, react defensively, attempt to talk over the complainer, or distract yourself with other business. Instead of telling yourself, "He can't talk to me like that," you should ask the patron, "Will you please tell me what needs to be done?" Using words like "situation" helps the customer to see you as a partner in mutual problem-solving and places you on common ground. (Calling it a complaint, or even a problem, can sometimes exacerbate a defensive posture on both sides, and it places the burden of proof and solution more heavily on the customer's shoulders.)

3. *Keep the conversation to a minimum.* You need to ask a combination of open and closed questions to clarify and understand what the complaint is about and to keep yourself and the customer focused on the facts rather than on the emotions involved. If the complaint is about the content of a book or other library materials, you should request that the customer put the complaint in writing. (Many libraries have a printed form for this purpose.) If a mistake on the part of the library is being reported, instead of reacting personally and saying, "You're not perfect. You make mistakes, too," respond professionally, and tell the patron, "This isn't the kind of service we want to provide. What can we do to correct the situation?" You need to convey a professional attitude.

4. *Respond positively, with a problem-solving approach.* Instead of telling yourself, *She* is attacking me, or *He* is accusing me of making a mistake, which inspires defensiveness, you need to ask yourself, "How can *I* resolve this situation?" Again, you should ask questions and restate the customer's responses for clarification. You should tell the patron what you *can* do rather than what you cannot do. You should also offer choices. Don't just restate policy; explain the reason *behind* the policy or procedure. Maybe you can't make an exception on the spot, but you can listen, get information from the patron, and offer to pass it

along to someone who might be able to effect a change. You should explore solutions with the customer and agree on what *each* of you will do. Let the customer know that he or she has come to the right person, and that you are there to help, not to create more frustration.

5. *Do what you have agreed to do.* If you need to get more information and call the customer later, you should do it promptly. And always thank the customer for talking with you about it.

The effective handling of customer complaints is a positive alternative to the win-lose battle. The goal of a library staff member is to provide first-class service to library users. This means working with users to solve problems without placing blame on anyone. Ultimately, *it does not matter who is right and who is wrong.* What really matters is your commitment to providing your customers, whenever possible, with what they want and need. The library's commitment to service and its relationship with its customers are what matters.

No matter how adept you become at handling complaints, you will never be able to make everyone happy. There are some people you will encounter for whom unhappiness with the world is a way of life. There is little you can do about these people's choices, including their choice to hold onto negative attitudes and to behave insultingly. By choosing to learn and practice excellent customer relations skills, you can enjoy the satisfaction of having done your best to provide first-class service to your customers, whether or not your treatment of their complaints results in a change in their behavior and attitudes. But it just might.

# THE CHRONIC COMPLAINER

While many complaints are justified and necessary, depending on the circumstances, there are some people for whom complaining seems to be a way of life. With these people, complaining is not simply a means of bringing a problem to the attention of someone who is in a position to do something about it. On the contrary, the chronic complainer (CC) may specifically *avoid* the person who might actually be able to help solve the problem. Instead, the complainer seeks to unload the complaint on someone who is perceived as less threatening to the complainer, someone who may be less involved in the problem than the complainer, someone who may in fact have *less* power to resolve it, but who, unfortunately, may appear willing to serve as a safe sounding board.

Certain behaviors are typical of CCs. They seek out anyone who is willing to listen, except the person who has the power to do something about the complaint. They whine, often talking on and on without pause in sentences that seem to have no periods at the end. They may accuse, blame, and find fault with the person who they claim to be the cause of their complaint, and who they view as more powerful than themselves. Their complaining may be associated with passive-aggressive motivations, but this connection is extremely difficult for the average person to spot. Consider the following scenario:

### Betty

Betty is employed as a paraprofessional in the children's services division of a large public library branch. Her immediate supervisor is Beverly, the children's librarian. Although there are only three full-time employees in the division, Beverly has a habit of communicating with Betty and Pat, the other paraprofessional, in written memos rather than through direct conversation, especially when the content concerns allocation of work assignments in the division.

Betty's work schedule does not coincide with that of her supervisor, and she frequently receives Beverly's memos when Beverly is not there to consult and clarify assignments. Betty interprets Beverly's brief, to the point, written directives as an exercise in power on the part of her supervisor. Betty would much rather participate in the decision-making about work assignments than receive the decision as a *fait accompli*. In her view, the inequality between herself and Beverly is made even more poignant by the lack of opportunity to respond immediately and face-to-face once she receives the memo. Over time, Betty becomes more and more sensitive to Beverly's behavior, interpreting much of her communicative style as a personal slight.

Betty feels angry, but not particularly hostile, about the situation in which she feels victimized, and she thinks Beverly ought to act and communicate in a way that would make her feel more equal. However, intimidated by her perception of Beverly's power, she fails to confront her supervisor with this collection of resentments. Instead, Betty is often seen sitting at the break table in the staff lounge, looking sad, worried, or annoyed, following the receipt of one of Beverly's directives.

Long-time staff members have learned to avoid showing concern toward Betty at these times for fear of getting trapped into listening. They have stopped asking her what's wrong, thereby adding their own contribution to Betty's feelings of woe. Kathy, the new adult reference librarian, however, is still in the introductory stages of Betty's game of "Alas" and has not yet learned to avoid getting hooked into playing "Why Don't You . . . Yes,But." Sincerely wanting to help, and not wishing to be insensitive, Kathy listens to Betty's complaints about Beverly and the library in general (e.g., "Why can't she *ask* me first before she makes these decisions?" "Nobody around here cares about anybody else but themselves!") She gives Betty her full attention, clucking sympathetically over Betty's victimization, then suggests that perhaps it would help if Betty approached Beverly about having a heart-to-heart talk, so she could let Beverly know how she felt ("Why don't you. . . ."). Betty responds that she has thought about that, but it would never work, since "she (Beverly) obviously doesn't like me" in the first place, and in the second place, such a conversation would place her (Betty) in an even more vulnerable position with Beverly. She really can't afford to alienate her supervisor, and "Beverly wouldn't understand anyway," and so on and so on ("Yes, But . . . ").

Racking her brain for other suggestions, such as talking to Pat about *her* experience with Beverly's management style, Kathy gets more and more frustrated as Betty dismisses each one ("I've tried talking to Pat, but she just makes excuses to leave the room. She's no help at all!") Eventually Kathy also gives up the struggle, feeling powerless to find a solution for Betty's problems and resentful at having been duped into listening. Determined not to get drawn into one of these frustrating conversations again, she often withdraws when she sees Betty coming. When she cannot leave, she tries to ignore Betty's whining and complaining and change the subject, until Betty finally withdraws (one expects, to find a more empathetic listener).

From Kathy's point of view, Betty has taken advantage of her good nature, and Kathy feels victimized by her. In fact, however, chronic complainers such as Betty often feel and behave like passive and powerless victims themselves a great deal of the time. Betty plays the game of "Alas," but she is not truly a passive-aggressive person. She needs attention and is attempting to get it in a non-hostile but passive way. In this passive state, CCs may credit their successes to chance or to the good graces of other people, rather than to their own abilities and efforts. In other words, they view their locus of control as existing somewhere outside of themselves.

## CONTROL AND ATTENTION AS COMPLAINT MOTIVATORS

To gain some measure of control over their lives, while avoiding personal responsibility for the outcome, they learn to play games such as "Alas" or "Why Don't You? . . . Yes, But. . . ." These two games often appear in sequence. The unwary listener is hooked into sympathizing with the complainer's woeful story, and the interaction dissolves into a game of "Why Don't You. . . ." Chronic complainers play these games for the same reasons that they avoid solving problems directly: They see others as somehow more powerful and responsible than they see themselves. Playing the game gives them some sense of control over their situation—in this case, by hooking the person perceived as more powerful into giving advice for action that is then rejected as impractical or impossible. The result, frequently, is more complaining, plus an active or passive veto of any suggestion that requires the CC to *do* something about the situation he or she is complaining about.

Control is not the only motivation of the chronic complainer. Although the griped-about problem does not get solved, the complainer does receive reinforcement for his or her behavior through the *attention* provided by the listener.

CCs are often Type IIIs; that is, they are analytical types who feel a sense of gratification in their ability to identify and diagnose a problem. Their ability to analyze what is wrong brings valuable thinking skills to a problem situation. Analytical persons have the ability to gather information, spot critical details that others might overlook, and respond to this critical information in ways that move the problem toward solution.

Type III complainers are often very competent at spotting problems. However, they become difficult by not focusing on the critical details and not using the information to solve the problem. Rather, in their victim role, CCs merely *notice* problems, then interpret them in a very personal, emotionally clouded way. They collect them, so to speak, and unload them on someone else when they become too much of a burden to carry alone. In their refusal to take action, and in the seeming willingness of other people to take on their burden for them (for awhile), CCs gain attention and reinforcement for their assumed nonresponsibility. By telling someone else what is wrong, they may feel they have done all they can. A secondary benefit of this strategy is that the complainer cannot be blamed, either for the problem or for the lack of an effective solution. In their eyes, those who have the power are responsible, both for the problem and for the solution.

## DEALING WITH THE CHRONIC COMPLAINER

In this section, you are moving beyond the handling of occasional complaints, and people you might not know personally, to dealing with people you might know quite well, or at least come into contact with regularly. These chronic complainers might include members of your family, friends, bosses, co-workers, and other people with whom you have some sort of short-term or long-term relationship. Their constant whining and complaining are usually well-known among their contacts who either try to avoid situations where they might get stuck hearing the latest round of complaints, or else endure the frustration of being their convenient victim.

From past experiences with difficult complainers, you may have concluded that paying attention and listening to these people does not work; therefore, conventional wisdom says that one should avoid them when they are in a complaining mode. Paradoxically, however, if CCs are unavoidable (as most library patrons and co-workers are), listening is exactly the place to begin to deal more effectively with their difficult behavior.

It is important to bear in mind that taking time to listen to a chronic complainer is not dysfunctional in itself. Rather, it is your tendency to take on responsibility for solving the complainer's problems that engage you in the game and sets you up for an impossible task. Changing your behavior and trying a new approach with any difficult person takes courage and commitment. You will probably not be successful the first time you try these new ways of interacting, but you might begin to see different responses from your difficult people if you are consistent in your behavior toward them over time. Remember, though: It is the responsibility of individuals to choose change for themselves. Any permanent change in another's attitude or behavior is beyond your control; you cannot coerce others into it or do it for them. You can only be responsible for what you are responsible for: namely, your own thoughts, needs, feelings, and behavior. Although chronic complainers can be seductive, you should not allow them, in effect, to delegate responsibility to you for solving their problems. Once you permit the monkey of responsibility on a complainer's back to leap onto your own shoulders, you are faced with inevitable frustration, failure, and diminished self-esteem.

Therefore, your goal in dealing with CCs is not to change their behavior but to take control of your *own*, while offering to help CCs change their behavior. If they choose to engage in problem-solving with you, they may also take the risk of changing their lives for the better.

The chronic complainer, as explained above, views his or her problems as an overwhelming burden and operates out of a position of helplessness, in which control over, and responsibility for, this position lies with someone else. While complainers may possess the analytical skills to spot problems, they may possess neither the confidence nor the skills necessary to determine which problems they can do something about. They need help in problem-solving, but first they need to know that someone really cares and sincerely wants to help. What a listener needs to do is to convey to the complainer that both persons are on the same team. The listener should convey a willingness to help bring the complaints out into the light of day, so to speak, where they can be clearly seen and understood, without the threat of negative consequences.

Therefore, the first step is to listen actively. This means that a listener, rather than try to escape or distract the complainer, needs to remove distractions and give full attention to what is being said. This may mean moving to a more private location and/or arranging a less-pressured time period to allow full exposition of the complaint. This initial active-listening posture and behavior signals that the listener is really trying to understand the problem.

*Understanding, however, is not the same as agreement.* Active listening, as you have seen, is accomplished in part by paraphrasing back to the speaker what you think he or she has said to you. It is crucial that the listener remain objective. What this means is that you must not appear to agree *or* disagree with the complaint. This can be extremely difficult to do, especially if you think that there is some merit to it. Agreeing with the complaint will not stop the complaining. Saying that you are sorry, or apologizing for the complainer's troubles will not work, either. Both agreement and apology, in fact, encourage *more* complaining rather than ending it, and they may be interpreted as willingness to take responsibility for solving the problem.

The goal in dealing effectively with the problem-bearing CC is to get him or her involved in the one thing he or she chronically avoids: solving problems. This may be hard at first, since the complainer is neither skilled nor accustomed to problem-solving. A few techniques can be used to get the person started in the process:

**Ask specific questions to get to the facts of the problem:** "Exactly what happened?" "Who was involved?" "When did this first occur?" "Where were you and X when it happened?" "Does everyone else see this as a problem?" You shouldn't ask a complainer why he or she believes such-and-such solution won't work. This merely puts him or her in a position of having to defend these beliefs and makes further conversation more frustrating and difficult for you as the listener. Remember, the key to clear, direct communication is to build bridges to a common ground, not to put up barriers and roadblocks.

**Provide structure for problem-solving:** Ask the complainer to describe the problem in writing and set a deadline for doing it. Or, when he or she starts getting into an endless string of woes, you should excuse yourself, get a pad and pencil, and start writing them down yourself. You will probably have to ask the complainer to start over and to slow down so that you can write it all down. This serves several purposes. First, it signals to the complainer that it is acceptable to proceed (although he or she may mistakenly assume that you plan to take responsibility for his or her woes). Secondly, it forces the complainer to think about his or her complaints instead of a well-rehearsed rote recitation of them. Thirdly, it prevents repetition of the same points over and over, since you can interrupt the complainer to indicate that the point has already been covered. Fourthly, it lets the complainer know that you are serious about his or her complaints and that you intend to help, but that you expect *the person* to do something. Finally, putting problems down on paper models a problem-solving technique that the complainer might try again sometime.

You can involve complainers further in the solution process by soliciting their ideas. But don't be surprised if they don't have any! After all, complainers do not routinely see problem-solving as being within their control or responsibility. Remember, CCs are often Type III analyzers at heart. Their goal is not to solve problems but to endlessly analyze and complain about them, since they have no real hope for actual change. However, when you give deadlines and ask for ideas, you set the complainer up for goal-setting (another problem-solving step).

**Provide structure for independent action:** By communicating your time limits, you let complainers know that you are willing to help but *not* willing to take responsibility for their problems. You should ask them to think about and tell you what they would like to accomplish as a result of your conversation. They may tell you that they want you or someone else to do something about their problems. On the other hand, you may be surprised to discover that, beneath the whining, the complainer actually *has* a goal. For example, Betty, in the above scenario, might respond:

> Oh, I don't know ... I guess I'd really like Beverly to communicate more personally with me about my work, you know, so that there could be more give-and-take in our relationship, so that I could have a better idea about how I'm doing.

An appropriate response to this is not only to be supportive but also to push for *action* on the complainer's part. However, rather than suggesting specific solutions, you should suggest a *method* of action to them. This might sound something like: "I can see this is important to you, and you certainly know a lot more about this situation than I do. Here is what I would recommend: Keep track of this problem in a journal for awhile. Document it in writing. Write down when it happens, who is present, where and how it happens, and what the result is. As you are keeping track of the problem, try to think of two or three things you could do to change the situation, or things you could do to solve the problem."

If the complainer is reluctant, tell him or her that the reason for writing things down is so he or she can see all the details and analyze them objectively. (Type IIIs do this naturally.) If you can, you should arrange to meet with the complainer again in a few days or a week to look at the details with him or her. Again, the deadline sets him or her up for goal-setting, and reassures the person that you are taking him or her seriously. Kathy's suggestion to Betty that she talk directly to Beverly about her communication style failed as part of the "Why Don't You . . . Yes, But . . . " game. However, once a listener has gotten a complainer engaged in the planning and problem-solving process (including seeing the listener as a partner in problem-solving rather than as a receptacle for problems), the same suggestion is far more likely to get a fair hearing and, perhaps, even a tryout, since it will come directly from the complainer.

**Give the complainer permission to take independent action:** You should tell complainers that you are glad to have had the conversation, and that they should let you know if they have any problems with the process you have proposed. At this point, complainers may protest lack of time or some other reason why they can't follow through with it. In that case, you can simply say, in a supportive way as they or you leave, "Well, if you change your mind, let me know."

There is no guarantee, of course, that CCs will seize control of their own powers or take responsibility for achieving solutions to their own problems, using the method and timeframe suggested. Indeed, they may simply cease complaining to you and look for someone new to play "Alas" with. On the other hand, a CC might choose to follow your suggestion by keeping track of the problem and thinking of solutions, or at least bring back information you can both review toward an eventual solution. In either case, your goal as the helpful listener is not to reform the chronic complainer but to cope more effectively with his or her difficult behavior in a way that allows you to feel good about yourself and your ability to do something positive to help another person. If others so choose, they might begin to take responsibility for solving their own problems and achieving their own goals.

# 3 DEALING WITH UNRESPONSIVE PEOPLE

Did I want to add anything? . . . I don't know . . . I guess not.

Oh, yes, I looked at the report. Comments? Well . . . We probably shouldn't do anything until we've gone over it more thoroughly. When? Gosh, I don't know. I've had a lot of other distractions lately. . . .

Difficult unresponsive people are often Type IVs whose dysfunctional behaviors fall into either or both of two modes, one characterized by silence and the other by indecision. Both types of unresponsiveness are strongly motivated by the Type IVs' typical desire to establish or maintain positive relationships with other people. They need the approval of others, and their primary motivating intention is to get along positively with other people. However, when these motivations are not accompanied by appropriate communication and decision-making skills, unresponsives can prevent them and others from making progress on important tasks and achieving worthwhile goals.

## THE SILENT UNRESPONSIVE

The old stereotype of the shushing librarian contains an element of truth. Silence is not generally considered by library staff to be problematic. However, silence *is* a problem if it is accompanied by behavior that is illegal (e.g., stealing), offensive to someone else (staring or stalking), or creates a barrier to getting some project moving or some task accomplished.

The latter type of silence, which will be discussed in this chapter, has more to do with people's *unresponsiveness* than with silence alone. When a person is unresponsive to our efforts to communicate, good service and good relationships become difficult to achieve, regardless of whether the person is a library user or a co-worker. Dealing with unresponsive people can be very frustrating, often more so than open conflict, since in conflict one at least has a chance of discovering the other person's real feelings, intentions, and goals. The closed-mouthed silent unresponsive (SU) provides none of this information. By being passive and silent, he or she thwarts all efforts to even identify needs and problems, let alone solve them. What can we do? We cannot coerce unresponsive people into talking with us. Use of superior power may yield temporary success but certainly doesn't encourage honesty and self-responsibility on the part of the other. However, it is essential that we try to get SUs to talk.

The only way we can determine how to handle our further interactions with them is to find out what is going on in their heads, what their needs and goals are, and what is keeping them from communicating. SUs may be silent and unresponsive for a number of reasons. Paradoxically, uncommunicative, unresponsive people are often overly concerned with maintaining good relationships with other people. Unfortunately, their behavior often provokes negative responses in spite of their good intentions because of the frustration and hostility it can lead to.

Usually, the operative emotion behind unresponsiveness is fear— fear of offending, fear of failure, fear of punishment. Silent, unresponsive people may be afraid that what they say might needlessly hurt someone, make waves, or otherwise cause discomfort to another individual or group. They may fear that if they say something, they will lose another's approval, they will be blamed, or someone will become upset and angry with them. So they refrain from giving information, stating opinions or disagreements, making decisions or commitments, or taking any action that might have a negative impact or draw a negative response from others. Rather than say anything that might offend someone, they don't say anything at all. This SU behavior pattern often has its foundations in childhood feelings and experiences with powerful adults, which are then evoked in current adult relationships.

Frequently the SU is a bright individual who, because of his or her analytical skills, is capable of perceiving potential problems that others may not. Perhaps this person has had the unhappy experience of having his or her warnings ignored, dismissed, or simply proven to be overstated. Wishing to avoid feeling misunderstood and unappreciated by others again, the SU offers no argument except silence, although the person might be silently saying to himself or herself something like, "Fine, do it your way. But when it goes wrong, don't tell me about it!"

On the other hand, sometimes people are reticent because they lack self-confidence in situations involving people whose status or power they perceive as greater than their own. Consider the case of Clem.

## Clem

Clem is a bright, polite, but not-too-confident young man who works in the library's small printing/graphics operations. Although Clem's formal education ended with high school, he enjoys reading and learning about computer hardware and software, uses them in his graphic design work, and has successfully helped several co-workers and friends acquire and set up personal computers. Because of his understanding and interests, Clem has been assigned to a task force to draw up specifications and choose new hardware and software capable of linking all staff members' desktop workstations in a local area network, and with the library's integrated acquisitions, cataloging, circulation, and accounting systems, in addition to word processing, database management, and electronic mail uses.

Margaret, the circulation librarian, is chair of the task force, which includes a variety of very articulate and opinionated professional and paraprofessional staff members. In each of the task force's meetings so far, Margaret has noticed that Clem has been silent the entire time. She knows Clem possesses a great deal of practical knowledge, and she has tried on several occasions to get Clem to participate actively in the discussion, but has she had no success in getting him to speak up. Guessing that Clem may be intimidated by this lively group, Margaret decides to talk with him privately. Clem arrives at the conference room promptly at the appointed hour. He seems somewhat nervous as he and Margaret exchange hellos then seat themselves at the conference table. Margaret needs to get Clem's perspective on the project, but she is worried that he still won't open up, even in a one-to-one setting.

## DEALING WITH THE SILENT, UNRESPONSIVE PERSON

The first thing to do when dealing with a person's unresponsive silence is, of course, to try to get the person to talk. This means *initiating the conversation* in a low-key, unpressured manner. To minimize pressure and potential frustration, you should allow enough time (say 15 or 20 minutes) with no interruptions which can let the SU off the hook.

*Small talk* can often help the SU person relax. However, small talk should not be extended beyond its usefulness in getting the person to say something. If carried on too long, trivial conversation just helps the person avoid talking about the very topic you want to discuss with him or her.

Once the person seems comfortable, it is time to begin *introducing the topic* into the conversation by making a brief, positive statement about it. You need not go into detail too much at this point. Then you should pause briefly. This signals the person that you are finished speaking and that a response is expected. If none is forthcoming, you should ask an open-ended question. Open-ended questions (usually beginning with "what") are those that require more than a yes or no or a one- or two-word response. (For example, "What do you think about what I just said?" or "How do you feel about that?" or "I'm interested in what you are thinking. Would you take a little time to describe it to me?") Then you should *be quiet* and allow the person time to respond.

This is the time to *let silence work* for you, instead of against you. The unresponsive person may need time to think about his or her answer. It should be clear to both of you that the conversational ball is in the SU's court. A way to reinforce this is to use appropriate body language to convey a message of anticipation. If sitting, you should lean forward. If standing, you should lean your head a little forward. You should look directly at the other person, your eyebrows raised, hands in front, palms-up, ready to hear what the person is about to say, and wait patiently but expectantly. Do not rush in to fill the silence, no matter how deafening it might seem. Getting other people to take up the conversational slack is a long-term behavior pattern for the silent unresponsive. Giving in to the temptation to talk is self-defeating.

Sometimes a question, followed by silence, will be enough to get the conversation rolling and focused on the topic you have raised. However, SUs are often experts on waiting out silences. If they remain silent, your next task is to *keep focused on the topic* you have raised while commenting in a non-accusatory way on their silence. For example, Margaret might say, "Clem, as I said, we need to move forward on this automation proposal. I thought we were going to talk about it, but you haven't said anything. What's going on?" If their reply is "Nothing," you should ask "What else?" If the reply is, "I don't know," you should say, "Guess." You may have to repeat this cycle if it doesn't work the first time. You should try to match the other person's posture to keep the conversation between equals. If the person is still silent, you may have to make a direct *request that he or she speak* ("Clem, please talk to me") or, if there has been some response, you should review what the person has contributed so far, no matter how insignificant.

(Caution: Do *not* ask, "Why won't you talk to me?" The unresponsive may not know why. The SU might interpret the "why" question as an accusation that he or she is doing something wrong and either respond defensively or withdraw completely.)

If nothing has worked so far, you should *attempt a guess* at what is going on in the SU's head. On target or not, an attempted guess at what is preventing him or her from talking, may just get him or her to open up, at least to correct a wrong guess. You should ask yourself (aloud) what would keep *you* from talking if you were in his or her position (e.g., "Concerns about your relationship?" "Fear about confronting or disagreeing with X?" "Afraid of making someone angry?" "An uncomfortable situation outside of the library?"). Then watch for a change (no matter how slight) in posture, movement, or eye contact that might signal that you are getting close to the right answer. Remember: The closer you come to stating what is going on in the other's mind, the more confident he or she will be that you really understand, and the safer the SU will feel about opening up.

If this still doesn't seem to be working, and if you feel yourself getting bogged down in the heaviness of the interaction, you should try to *ease some lightness, even humor, into the situation*. Getting the other person to relax and laugh will allow both of you the time and space to regroup and try again. Use of this technique with children and teenagers is especially effective.

As a last resort, you can let the person know that you *respect his or her privacy*, but that his or her remaining silent will eventually erode your relationship or destroy the team's chance for success. For the SU who is mainly concerned about maintaining good relationships (Type IV), this may be just the extra push needed.

*You should appeal to the person's sense of responsibility to provide information that will be damaging in the future if over-looked.* ("You have a much better grasp of details that we may have overlooked. I really need you to level with me now, before we get so deep into this project we can't change direction.")

If any of these steps prompt a response, you need to congratulate yourself (silently, of course). If not, *end the conversation* in order to avoid further frustration. However, it is important not to let the unresponsive person off the hook. Do not reinforce the silent behavior with warmth. Let the person know, in a business-like way, that you *intend to bring up the topic again*, and ask him or her to meet with you later. But you should not simply leave it to *some other time*. Always suggest a specific time in the near future so that he or she knows you intend to follow through, and ask the person to call you to confirm the time. Then you should say, "See you later." Once an SU knows that you are determined to get his or her ideas and opinions sooner or later, the SU may choose sooner, and begin to open up. ("Well, I guess I do have some thoughts about it.") If this happens, sit down with the person and proceed with the conversation, remembering to use active listening to keep him or her talking.

You may have tried consistently and persistently to no avail to get a subordinate SU to talk. If you have reason to believe that the person's silence is a form of Type II passive-aggression, sabotage, or insubordination, you may have to resort to some type of disciplinary action, with the guidance of the library's personnel or grievance policies and procedures. If so, you should let the person know that you intend to take action and what he or she can expect. But you should be sure also to let the person know that you would much prefer that the individual talk with you and avoid official action. Give the person one more chance to make a productive and face-saving choice. It might just work.

# THE INDECISIVE UNRESPONSIVE

People who can't make up their minds can be frustrating no matter what their status but especially if they are in positions of authority. They may be quite congenial and encouraging. Unlike the silent unresponsives, they are often highly communicative—until it comes to making a decision. They will go to great lengths to stall and stonewall, just to avoid upsetting anyone.

Indecisive unresponsives (IUs) are usually people-focused Type IVs, rather than task-focused, and passive rather than aggressive in their communication style. They prefer to let other people make decisions whenever possible.

This can be a good style to cultivate, especially for someone in a parental or mentor role. It offers safety and protection for the child or the fledgling manager, for example, while allowing him or her to develop strength and confidence in decision-making, through experiencing the consequences of his or her decisions. However, when one is not in a parental or mentor role, this *difficult* style, taken to an extreme, is counterproductive. The IU needs to be making the decisions, not fostering decision-making in someone else. Consider the following scenario:

### Kathy and Dorothy

Three weeks ago, Karen, head of the library's adult services unit, presented a draft of a written proposal for a new adult literacy service to Dorothy, the library director, in response to Dorothy's request. Karen and her staff worked many extra hours developing the proposal, which is very thorough. Karen needs Dorothy's approval to move ahead with the project.

About a week after giving it to the director, Karen asked Dorothy if she had had a chance to read the proposal and said that she was eager to hear any comments Dorothy might have for improvement. Dorothy replied that she had been very busy that week, but that yes, indeed, she had skimmed through it, and it looked very good.

However, Dorothy continued, she needed to find some time to go back and read it more carefully before getting back to Karen on it. That was two weeks ago. The proposal is still sitting on Dorothy's desk. When the subject comes up, she assures Karen that she will respond "soon." Karen thinks Dorothy is stalling because there is something seriously wrong with the proposal, or has changed her mind about the need for the new service. ("Why doesn't Dorothy just tell me what it is so I can fix it or forget about it?")

What is going on here? Actually, Dorothy did devote considerable time to reading the proposal shortly after it was presented to her. There is nothing substantively wrong with it. Dorothy feels that such a program is sorely needed in the community, and that documented evidence of that need ought to be emphasized more in the section on justification, in order to persuade the board to fund it. She also feels that the costs of some budgeted items are a bit unrealistic, and that the whole document could benefit from some reorganization and tightening up. Why hasn't she shared her reflections with Karen (who is running out of patience with Dorothy and out of enthusiasm for the project)?

Dorothy is preventing herself from taking action on the proposal because she is too concerned about Karen's feelings and the feelings of her staff. *Smooth relationships are paramount* to Dorothy, a classic Type IV. For extreme "relaters" like her, any expression of criticism (even when it is repeatedly requested), or any important decision, has the potential to annoy, discourage or disappoint someone. Dorothy sees the role of director as one of helping, encouraging, and cheering her employees on to success. Giving negative feedback makes her very uncomfortable, so she has developed the habit of avoiding it whenever possible. She sometimes denies the existence of problems to herself and avoids the responsibility of making decisions, so as not to hurt people. She may be unaware that she is rationalizing to herself: "Maybe if I wait a little longer the problem will solve itself or go away." Meanwhile she continues to listen to others, reassure and encourage them, and offer support and assistance.

## DEALING WITH THE INDECISIVE PERSON

The first thing Karen needs to do with Dorothy is to find out what is on her mind.

As with the clam-like silent unresponsives, indecisives are kept from responding as you need them to do by some internal conflict. If they are to make and commit themselves to a decision, you need to *create a safe environment* for them. Pushing harder with these difficult people will merely put them on the defensive or force them to withdraw, which is self-defeating for you and excruciating for them (since relating is so important to them). Therefore, you should slow down. By slowing down the pace of your conversation and general approach to them, you will, paradoxically, have a better chance of moving ahead with indecisives. Type IV relaters feel more comfortable and respond more honestly if you keep to their pace and emphasize the relationship rather than the task (feedback and decision-making). You should keep underscoring the idea that their honesty will enhance the climate of teamwork within the library and make relationships stronger.

Dorothy is avoiding giving criticism, so Karen could say, "Dorothy, you have said some really encouraging things about the proposal I gave you. But any project like this has some good points and some that aren't so great. It would really help me, Dorothy, if you could tell me about some of those areas that aren't quite as good as they could be. Even if they aren't that important, I would really like you to tell me about them." Indecisives really want to be helpful. Framing their doubts and criticism in a different way, as something that will *help*, will enable them to focus on your *task*, rather than on not hurting your feelings. It will help them to overcome their internal conflict by making their expression of negative information congruent with their need to help and relate positively with you.

Note carefully what they say. They may try to minimize the importance of their negative points, but realize that these points are important—so important, in fact, that these points have kept the indecisives from being open and honest with you from fear of upsetting you. Once you find out what is really on these persons' mind, you can begin to think of alternatives that will overcome and resolve these misgivings and move them closer to a decision.

It is important to stay in a low-pressure, relating mode with the IU. (This may be challenging if you are more task-oriented than relationship-oriented yourself, but perseverance will yield its rewards.) If the IU still seems reluctant to level, you should work with them to *clarify what is holding them back* or whom they are afraid of offending. Keep emphasizing how their honesty will truly help you, and that it is OK for them to tell you.

When you feel that they have honestly revealed both their positive and negative thoughts to you, you should *help them make a decision* by working through the process with them. Assist them in weighing the options and making choices. You can do this by suggesting that you both make a list of the possible alternatives (writing them down), then examining them one by one. Together, you can consider the probable consequences, both favorable and unfavorable, of each alternative. Are the best consequences worth the risk of the worst? Could you live with that?

You may feel yourself getting more intense at this stage of the process, but you shouldn't put pressure on indecisives to make a decision before you find out what their fears and reservations are. You want a rational decision you can both live with, not an emotional one you may both live to regret later.

Remember that the extremely indecisive person may never have developed the skills necessary to make effective decisions. Other people's approval is such a strong motivator that the person may have never learned how to be decisive. By working through this process with him or her, at a safe pace, you are modeling how rational decisions are made and empowering the IU to make them. If you continue over time to create a safe environment for honesty, if you model this behavior and help him or her work through the process, the IU will eventually start doing it on his or her own (which was your goal to begin with).

Once the IU learns how to make a decision, and does so, you should *clarify what the decision means in terms of further action*. List the specific action steps in order ("Ok, first you are going to send a memo to the staff, then you're going to . . . , etc., etc.") Be supportive of the decision, giving reassurance that it will work out and that he or she has made the right choice. You can give help with some of the action steps so that the person won't feel overwhelmed or alone in carrying out a commitment to action.

Finally, since you are dealing with a people-oriented person, you need to work to *reinforce your relationship with an IU*. You should open up and give honest feedback. Continue to create a safe climate for honesty. Affirm and appreciate an IU's honesty, whenever it is offered, and let the person know that it is his or her honesty that will continue to *enhance* your relationship. ("Dorothy, I'm so glad you told me what the proposal really needed. It was so helpful. I really enjoy working with someone I can count on to be honest.") When you encourage people to be honest, when you sincerely appreciate their efforts at honesty, you are likely to see more of it in their speech and behavior. And everybody wins!

# 9 DEALING WITH YES-PEOPLE AND NO-PEOPLE

I know . . . you did say you needed that data for today's meeting. What can I say . . . . Hey, how's that decorating project coming along? . . . Good! What? Oh, the data . . . How about next Tuesday? I'll have it ready for you first thing Tuesday morning!

## THE DIFFICULT AGREEABLES

As we have seen in the previous chapter, honesty may be the best policy in dealing with the person who is either indecisive or silently unresponsive. For most of us, of course, honest communication on the part of other people can, from time to time, be a mixed blessing. While an honest opinion can certainly help correct a problem before it becomes worse, or move us in a more positive direction, it can also be difficult or painful sometimes to listen to. This is especially true if we are inclined to interpret another's honesty as a negative. We can all think of instances when we have had our feelings hurt by someone's passive-aggressiveness disguised as honesty. On the other hand, there may have been times when we wished someone had saved us a great deal of frustration and time by being honest and pointing out the error of our chosen path.

### UNDERSTANDING THE YES-PERSON

Practicing genuine honesty—that is, sharing our view of reality openly with another without an ulterior motive—can sometimes be just as difficult as receiving it. Why should this be so? Why do people sometimes tell us what they think we *want* them to say instead of telling us what they truly believe or feel? Why do they make promises to do something, like meet a deadline, and then fail to keep the promise?

These frustrating little examples of dishonesty are associated (paradoxically) with the yes-person (YP) and his or her habitual need to relate positively with others. These are Type IV (relater-type) people who are strongly other-people-oriented. They tend to have a powerful need for approval of others, especially those who have authority over them or whom they perceive as more powerful than themselves in important ways. This inequality of power is not

**105**

limited to physical aspects alone. Ultra-agreeable YPs may defer to others whom they see as experts, as having more skill or talent in some area, or simply as more well known. They may transfer the recognized authority or superiority of someone in a single area of ability or effort into areas where it simply does not exist—for example, the movie star or sports hero who haunts the talk shows with wisdom and advice on how to get the most out of life. These relater-type people genuinely like people and want them to feel good. In a YP's efforts to get along and get approval, he or she, like the indecisive, may be reluctant to voice even minor objections for fear of hurting the other person's feelings or appearing negative.

We all do this occasionally. Someone (a friend, a family member, a patron, or the boss) needs something done, and, to please the individual, we promise or even volunteer to do it, only to get sidetracked by other concerns. Or we agree to do something by such-and-such deadline, only to discover that the task is much more complex or time-consuming than we had thought. Sometimes we resolve this problem by admitting that our expectations were unrealistic and renegotiating what we can realistically do to help. However, some people are more prone to procrastinate. Indeed, procrastination often begins this way. We are involved in something that is more difficult or time-consuming than we are comfortable with. So we distract ourselves by doing something else that we are comfortable with, or that we know how to do well (e.g., eating instead of studying, watching TV instead of writing, day-dreaming instead of working). This is what happens when we agree to do something, then end up making excuses for not doing it.

With YPs, this happens habitually. However, their excuses and their genuine desire to please make it difficult for others to stay angry at them. They may appear to have boundless energy—to be constantly busy, moving and talking—but their activity amounts to so much wheel-spinning. Their motto seems to be, "Promise them anything—they'll love you for it!"

### Bill

Bill's new duties as assistant director include editing a monthly newsletter that publicizes recent acquisitions and upcoming library events. At a staff meeting, each branch and department head agreed to provide Bill with timely written information by a stated deadline each month. For the last five months, the process has worked smoothly, except where Gerry is concerned. Gerry's department is responsible for a large share of the public service programming for the library, and Bill has had to contact Gerry repeatedly, month after month, to get the information he needs to go to press since Gerry *never* delivers on time. Most of the time, Bill ends up having to write down the information himself as Gerry dictates it to him over the phone. It seems as though Gerry is extremely preoccupied with getting her programs together, and that she either doesn't care or just isn't organized enough to get the information together for Bill.

Bill is getting so frustrated with Gerry's apparent lack of commitment to follow through and meet the deadlines that he is tempted to just leave Gerry's department out of the newsletter entirely and feature those departments that do cooperate. However, he knows that such a solution would be unacceptable to everyone, particularly the director and the customers who regularly attend and support Gerry's programs. Besides, Gerry is such a *nice person*! She always apologizes profusely when Bill calls, claiming circumstances beyond her control as an excuse (e.g., "You know how it is around here sometimes. I really meant to do it, but so many other things came up." Or, "The phone just never stopped ringing this week!"). She begs his forgiveness and promises to get her information in early next month. Gerry always goes out of her way when she sees him to ask Bill about his family and seems to take a genuine interest in whatever project he is working on. How could he be angry with her? Bill senses no hostility or attempted sabotage from Gerry whatsoever. Rather, she is one of the friendliest people he has ever met. He doesn't want to get Gerry or himself in trouble with anyone. But he is stumped about her false promises and apparent lack of commitment to his newsletter publication deadlines. What can he do?

## THE FOCUS ON RELATIONSHIPS

Remember that YPs are focused on *relationships* with other people, on getting along and not hurting others' feelings. They are difficult because they are not focused on the *task* we want them to do, which might vary from giving us an honest opinion to carrying out some promised action. Rather than risk losing our friendship, they make commitments they cannot possibly carry out, given their weakness in planning skills and time management. To evade our anger or displeasure with them, they go out of their way to let us know how much they like and approve of us.

In this regard, our goal in dealing with this overly agreeable, "promise 'em anything" type of person is very similar to our goal in dealing with the unresponsive or indecisive person: *to help them make commitments and follow through on them.* To do this requires a commitment on our part to show appreciation for their good intentions but also to honestly explore their lack of follow through with them, and to offer our partnership in the development of a realistic plan of action that will make us both winners.

## DEALING WITH YES-PEOPLE

First, you need to *create a safe environment for honesty*. There are a number of ways of communicating the idea that it is alright to be honest, including making a direct statement to that effect. However, habitual YPs are already operating on their own internal cues that it is not safe for them to express objections or disagreements. To break through this barrier, a slower, more indirect, subtle approach will probably work more effectively. The indirect approach includes both verbal and nonverbal elements.

**Non-Verbal:** Whenever you are in the yes-person's presence, even if you are not directly involved in a conversation with him or her, you should try consistently to *reflect his or her non-verbal behavior with your own*. For example, if you are in a meeting with a YP, and the person leans forward, you should lean forward. If he or she is doodling on paper, you should begin to doodle, too. If he or she plays with a pen, you should do the same. However, take care not to make your behavior too noticeable or obvious. The goal is for the YP to receive the *unconscious* nonverbal message that you are "in sync" with him or her, that you can be trusted, that you have common interests, and that you want to work with the YP cooperatively. (Of course, you will want to balance your participation in the meeting with your awareness of the YP's non-verbal responses.)

**Verbal:** When you interact with YPs verbally, you should also *try an indirect approach*. Remember that these persons have a strong need for approval and want to get along. You can provide acceptance of YPs as people and safety and support for their honesty by being people-focused and considerate yourself. Instead of saying, "I," or, "You," you can try using more inclusive pronouns like "we" and "us." Speak in terms of "our" department, newsletter, or library, to help the person know you consider them a part of the team. Instead of starting right in on your agenda when you meet a YP, you should ask him or her, "Is this a good time for us to talk?" All these methods communicate the message that you want your relationship with the person to be strong, respectful, and cooperative, that his or her unconscious fear of hurting or of being punished is unfounded, and that it is safe for the YP to be honest with you.

As with the indecisives, your next goal is to get the YP to *focus more on the task* at hand and less on the relationship. Yes people are difficult because, among other things, they habitually promise to deliver but don't follow through. Deadlines come and go with nothing to show for them except excuses and more promises. Such experiences with YPs indicate that they are full of good intentions but probably have no clear idea of what actually needs to be done. Because their excuses and promises have worked so well for them in the past, their skills in planning and organizing tasks for themselves may be weak to nonexistent. Therefore, you will have to work through the process with them. This means being specific about the task you want them to accomplish, laying it out piece-by-piece, step-by-step, and being clear about priorities—that is, which parts are most important and need to be done first.

When you are setting priorities, it helps to think of tasks in terms of how much time is involved, how difficult they are, and what rewards are attached to them. For the YP (as for many of us), *starting* is the most formidable obstacle. Once you have some momentum going, the rest of the job seems to flow with its own energy. A rule of thumb, then, is to do first the task that either is the most time-consuming, is the most difficult, or has the most potential for reward.

- *Doing the most time-consuming part first* makes everything else seem to go faster.
- *Doing the most difficult part first* makes everything else seem easier.
- *Doing the most rewarding thing first* provides the early payoff that keeps the momentum going during the rest of it.

Along with priorities, the YP must understand the task in terms of *sequence*. This means not only that the job is broken into smaller pieces, but also that the path from part one to part two to part three, etc., is clear and makes sense in terms of the time allotted. In other words, if Gerry tells Bill she will have the newsletter information to him by the end of the day, Bill might say, "Wonderful! How much do you think you can give me by noon?"

Helping the person learn to plan and organize a task also includes *dealing with excuses*. For example, Gerry frequently uses her constantly ringing telephone as a excuse for not getting things done. The telephone and other interruptions by people are often a problem for everyone in libraries, but a suggested solution would be schedule a period of an hour or two several times a week for quiet concentration. You should tell others that you need to concentrate for awhile and ask someone else to take phone messages (or get an answering machine, if that would be appropriate in the work setting). Or you could schedule specific times for answering your phone, and tell people when is the best time to call.

If you cannot work behind a closed door, you can tell people who stop by to chat that you are trying to meet a deadline and that you would appreciate it if you could get back with them later when you can give them your full attention. When you *promise undivided attention later*, you let people know that you consider their needs to be important, and your sincere request will help you keep the interruptions to a minimum.

This tactic may be difficult for YPs to implement. However, if they can see how interruptions eat away at their time to get the task done, it may motivate them to try it, especially if they can look forward to talking with the interrupter (a Type IV intent) without having to worry about the unfinished task or looming deadline.

Working *with* the yes-person, to teach and help him or her plan tasks and prioritize time, is a gift that builds strong and safe working relationships. This is just what YPs want and need, and it is the key to reciprocity and commitment to a task on their part which is what you want and need from them.

Before leaving the person to perform the task, though, you should ask him or her to *summarize specifically what it is the person plans to do*. Keep clarifying and reinforcing the steps in the plan and the timeframes you have agreed upon until you are convinced that both of you are thinking along the same track. You should ask—*not demand*—that the person put the plan in writing in some way (e.g., on his or her schedule or in a memo). Asking a YP to write it down makes the plan more concrete and increases the likelihood of its getting done. Asking for written confirmation does not mean you do not trust the person to follow through. Rather, you should emphasize, that it provides the individual with a written record of what needs to be done and the timeframe for doing it.

To guarantee a YP's commitment to following through on the task, you do not merely settle for a promise. *Appeal to their sense of honor and desire to maintain the relationship.* Ask, "Do you really mean that?" "Can I really count on you to do what you've promised?" "Do you really think you can get it to me by four o'clock?"

Again, with a Type IV-relater like this (people who need people), the relationship is the key to getting commitment and action on the task. It is well worth the minimal time and effort needed to continue building and maintaining that relationship, by taking an interest in the person and his or her life beyond the tasks you want done. You need to let YPs know you appreciate their honesty, especially when they express doubts and concerns about what you want them to do, or about the feasibility of our deadlines. Explore their concerns with them and help them to draw up a plan of action that you both agree is realistic and will move the task forward.

# THE DIFFICULT DISAGREEABLES

Job sharing? It just won't work. It would be a waste of time to try. People are just too resistant to changing things here. Why even bother thinking about it.

The ability and willingness to say "no" to other people when we are unable or unwilling to comply with their requests and demands is a healthy attitude worth cultivating. As seen in the previous chapter, being honest means sharing our objections and concerns when the task and the relationship at hand call for it, and this sometimes means pointing out the negatives in the situation. Saying "no" for these reasons can be helpful both to us and to others. However, there are people whose nay-saying is neither healthy nor helpful. The dynamics of dealing with these difficult "no-people" (NPs) will be explored next.

The negativist or "no-person" is virtually at the opposite end of the spectrum (both figuratively and literally) from the "yes-person." NPs are not the hostile or aggressive people we explored in earlier chapters. Rather, no-people are peculiar examples of extreme Type III behavior. They are the negativists, the eternal pessimists, always expecting the worst to happen. They can be counted upon to see the dark side of everybody's motives or to take a negative view of just about every situation or problem that involves them, and their "What's the use? Why bother?" futile attitude can leave those around them feeling desperate and hopeless. They chronically counter other people's enthusiasm with gloom and doom. When challenged to explain their reasoning, they respond, "What would be the point?"

## UNDERSTANDING THE NO-PERSON

Unlike the super-agreeable yes-person, the NP is not a relater-type. Rather, the negativist is someone who is quite *task*-oriented and *analytical* (Type III). He or she often has a highly developed ability to notice the minutest details. The difficultly with the NP lies in his or her habitual attention to the dark side of things. NPs can tell us more than we ever wanted to know about why our opinion is wrong, why our plan won't work, or why an action is not worth doing. As much as the Type IV yes-person seems eternally optimistic and full of interpersonal energy (although misdirected), the Type III no-person can actually *drain* us of energy. If we spend too much of our time and energy trying to get a positive response from no-people, we run the risk of becoming negative like them. They have the curious ability to trigger the propensity for fear and hopelessness that exists in every human heart.

It can be extremely difficult to maintain morale with no-people in the group, because the locus of control over their lives is somewhere outside themselves. They see their relationship with management (indeed, with authority figures in general) as "us versus them," and they rarely trust people whom they perceive as more powerful than themselves. They may look and feel chronically depressed.

How did they get to be this way? While you may never be able to trace the exact evolution of our particular NP's negative style, he or she probably has a history of being constantly disappointed by persons who are or were emotionally important in some way. The negativist is someone who may have been a particularly bright and curious child at one time but over the years has learned that trusting people only leads to heartache. No-people, beneath the apparent anger and bitterness with the hand fate has dealt them, are well-meaning and competent. But their view of reality inspires them to dash the dreams and wishes of others in order to *save* them from the pain and disillusionment the NP believes are inevitable. Analytical but passive by nature, NPs have a strong need for accuracy and a deep desire to see themselves, and to be seen, as correct. It is not that they dislike others. It is just that they see life as depressing, and they feel an obligation to tell others just how life *really* is, while protecting themselves from disappointment by maintaining emotional distance from others.

## DEALING WITH NO-PEOPLE

Being in the presence of a no-person for any extended time can drag you down toward their level if you do not take some precautions. One obvious safeguard is to avoid the negativist if you can. For most of us, though, complete avoidance of these difficult people is not an option. If you must interact with a no-person, the most important thing to do first is to make up your mind that you will *maintain a positive perspective* regardless of what the negativist says. You should expect the chronic NP to reinforce your sunny attitude. No-people habitually see the downside of everything. Their pattern is to discourage, not to encourage. This is why they are considered difficult. So you need to keep your own realistic but optimistic perspective by reminding yourself that the negativist's problems and attitudes are the result of the negativist's experience. *Your experience, and what you have learned from it, is different.* You know that sometimes bad things happen to the best of you (including having to deal with negative people), but you learn to survive and find joy in life just the same.

Because you cannot expect to be emotionally nourished by NPs, you must *take care of your own needs*, even if they cannot, by countering their negativisms with positive, but reasonable, statements of your own. This does not mean that you should argue with an NP or try to prove him or her wrong. NPs already are convinced they are right, and they will discount contradictory facts. You will never be able to convince them otherwise by using logic. In fact, they are probably the victorious veterans, at least from their own perspective, of many of these futile battles, although they derive very little joy from their victories. ("Don't get your hopes up, and you won't be let down.")

Rather than reacting in kind to the NP's negative viewpoint, you should simply breathe deeply and allow yourself time to *respond from your own perspective, not theirs.* Rather than arguing or trying to persuade the negativist to see things from your point of view, you can acknowledge the merits of what they have to say, without either agreeing or disagreeing. For example, you might say, "You know, Mary, there's a lot of truth in what you've just said. I used to feel like nothing was ever going to turn out the way I wanted it to, that there would always be something or someone who would come along to spoil things for me." Then you can add, "But you know, I decided to focus on what I *could* do instead of what I couldn't, and I found out I had a lot of things going for me. I guess I consider myself pretty lucky. I think I've got a lot of blessings to be thankful for." You might even begin to list some of those "blessings." What this does is keep *you* in a positive frame of mind. In a group situation, making positive statements like this can *help others maintain a positive outlook* and keep everyone from being dragged down by the no-person. The negativist can divert people's energy into a downward spiral. Modeling a positive attitude through positive statements can provide a healthy alternative to the negativism and get energy moving forward toward discovering productive solutions to problems. Such behavior allows you to keep a healthy emotional distance from the no-person while still interacting.

When you must engage in conversation with the NP, you should remind yourself that everyone, the negativist included, must have *something* to offer, even if it is just an opportunity for you to build strength of character! Again, instead of disagreeing or trying to cheer up the no-person who is warning you about problems, you can *try active listening*. Acknowledge and repeat back to the person what you hear him or her saying. Help the NP to explore his or her gloomy predictions in specific detail.

You can get the most out of the negativist's responses by using his or her analytical abilities to your advantage. Because NPs are so task-oriented, and because they are always looking for problems, they often are able to spot them before anyone else notices. NPs can actually make a positive contribution to your efforts by giving you an opportunity to handle problems and make corrections early on. In the process you will maintain your positive perspective and, perhaps, empower the negativists to think about their ability to control things in a different way.

Remember, most Type III no-people are not hostile. Behind the protective armor of negativistic behavior, they may truly care about and want to protect other people from experiencing the same hurts and disappointments they have had. If you *assume that their intentions are positive* even if their behavior is not, you might be able to get their frame of reference to deviate a little from its ordinary position. You can put a new twist on their responses. You can try saying something like, "I really appreciate the fact that you care so much about (this project, the people here, etc.)." This is not what NPs are used to hearing. It will most certainly cause them surprise and/or confusion and get their attention for what you have to say next. "It's pretty obvious to me that you care very much about it. I mean, why would you be so concerned about telling us what's wrong with it if you didn't want us to get it right?" To be right is what an analytical Type III person wants and needs. By seeing the positive intention behind negativists' behavior (even if it is only assumed), we may succeed in getting them to admit it to themselves, and eventually to others.

Getting negativists to view their own intentions as positive is a stepping stone to persuading them (perhaps) to be more flexible in their behavior. However, if things do seem to be improving as a result of your no-person's contributions, you might *ask them to try focusing on what people are doing right* instead of what they are doing wrong, "just to see what would happen." Caution: You may never be able to get an NP to acknowledge the good points in a person or a plan instead of the bad ones. But there is always a possibility that he or she might try it. If so, be sure to *point out the change in behavior to other people*. Subtle positive feedback from yourself and others can work wonders to reinforce further movement towards the positive on the part of no-persons. As they begin to see themselves in a more positive light, NPs gain more power to take control and effect further change in their lives.

If these methods fail, you can always *try reverse psychology*. This requires basically good intentions and some convincing acting ability on your part but may actually work with the die-hard negativist who consistently contradicts people and their ideas. The trick is for you to think of all the possible negatives *ahead of time* then present them to the NP as *negatively* as you can. He or she may surprise you by *contradicting* your negatives with what are essentially positive solutions to your problem. If this works, you should keep it up, and you may even be able to get the NP to devise a plan to counteract your *hopelessness* or to talk you into a more positive attitude. If this happens, you shouldn't forget to thank and *reward the no-person for caring and helping*. Persistence on your part may result in a gentle but definite shift in perspective of his or her part.

Remember, analytical Type III people, such as NPs, want to be appreciated for being right. Even if a project succeeds despite their negativism, you should be sure to include them in the celebration, as if they were a part of the winning team all along. If you do this consistently, they may begin to think of themselves as a part of the team, too.

# 10 KNOW-IT-ALLS

*Now ... is everyone clear on why we're not going to start circulating videos? I just don't foresee enough demand to justify the cost. Besides, we can use the money to add to our cassette tape collection much more cheaply.*

Make no mistake—expert knowledge is an asset to be treasured. Working with people who are experts in their fields can provide us with numerous opportunities to learn and grow. The more we know about things that are important to us, the more valuable they can be. Knowledge in itself is not the problem with the difficult persons we will be exploring in this chapter. Rather, as we have seen time and time again, the problem is more likely to be related to the habitual behavioral and communication style of a particular type of knowledgeable individual. Robert Bramson has labeled this type of expert the "Bulldozer."[1] For purposes of this discussion, we will refer to him or her as the "True Know-It-All" (TKIA).

## TKIA BEHAVIOR

TKIAs really are experts on some things. But not all experts are TKIAs. Many experts fully recognize their own limits and that, indeed, they do not know *everything*. They understand that much of their success depends on the cooperation of others, and they are often quick to share credit where it is due. They may or may not be famous, but they most certainly have been recognized at one time or another for their expertise. Through determination, study, and experience, they have accumulated an impressive and intensive body of knowledge in certain narrow areas of interest and, in the process, usually have acquired a wide smattering of conversational knowledge in many other areas. They may have achieved positions of power by this route, and may often be called upon to solve difficult problems. Understanding their own limits, however, they know instinctively when to call on other experts for advice. Here is where the similarity between most experts and TKIAs ends.

The difficulty TKIAs provide for other people lies in the fact that they frequently and habitually act *as if* they know everything, which they do not, and in the "steamroller" manner in which they treat the knowledge and opinions of others. Their treatment of others has more to do with their basic needs and intentions than with their expertise, of course. TKIAs are basically Type IIs, task-

**117**

oriented rather than people-oriented, and they are more generally more assertive than passive. More often than not, when it comes to their true areas of expertise, they *do* know what they are talking about. However, their need to constantly reinforce their position of power through knowledge can get in the way of their productively interacting with clients, colleagues, and others. In some ways they resemble (in their efforts to be in control of interactions with other people) the Type II hostile-aggressive types discussed earlier. However, TKIAs rely less on overtly hostile methods of gaining and preserving control than they do on intimidating and manipulating others into recognizing their great knowledge. They accomplish their goals through a combination of highly predictable behaviors, such as demanding that their solution to a problem or their way of doing something be seen as the *only* effective one, cutting off or minimizing alternative solutions or methods offered by others (especially others who are younger or less powerful), and maintaining distance (either physical or emotional) from others with knowledge or experience that is *inferior* to theirs.

TKIAs often want everyone to do things their way, within their timeframe, and with the same degree of skill as they possess. To an enlightened observer, they seem threatened by ideas that are different from their own, and by people who are different from them in appearance and background. In sharp contrast to the Type IV SUs or IUs, TKIAs not only appear certain that they know all the answers, they also become upset if anyone should challenge the feasibility of their solution or plan of action. TKIAs seem to care very little that others may also be knowledgeable and have something to contribute, including information that may lessen the validity of the TKIA's *facts*. They tend to be so closed-minded to new information that, if something does go wrong with their solutions, TKIAs may either blame someone else's inadequacies or offer intricate rationalizations showing that the failure could not possibly be their fault.

Remember that TKIAs are basically highly productive and worthwhile people with many admirable qualities. They have the potential to be very effective leaders because of their intense personal energy, persistence in overcoming problems, and self-motivation. It is the steam-roller aspects of their behavior that are problematic, and that leave others feeling frustrated, with lowered self-esteem and doubt about their own competency. TKIAs set up barriers to communication, either intentionally or inadvertently, through their condescending tone and inattention to others' feelings and ideas. They often respond to others' questions and doubts with irritation, defensive retreat, or out-and-out hostility, interpreting them as personal attacks when, in fact, others are just trying to understand them better. When this happens, TKIAs cling even more strongly to their solutions and plans and may compulsively pursue a course of action even when it is obvious to everyone else that the course will end in failure.

This style of extreme Type II behavior leaves other people feeling excluded and confused, if not downright stupid. Such constant discounting of our opinions and questions can discourage us from even trying to contribute anything to the discussion, which will usually be dominated by the TKIA anyway.

## HOW DID THE TKIA GET THIS WAY?

While it would be impossible to trace the evolution of every TKIA's behavior from childhood to adulthood, there are a number of assumptions that seem to logically explain the TKIA frame of reference. One is that TKIAs are strongly motivated to learn as much as they can and to organize their body of acquired knowledge in such a way as to enable them to feel secure in the world as they have experienced it. To them, the more they know, the more certain they are of their facts and how they fit together, the more capable they will be of surviving in a world that often seems chaotic. While others have learned that people and events outside of themselves are largely uncontrollable and unpredictable, and have learned to cope (and even find joy) by spontaneously going with the flow, TKIAs cope very poorly with the ambiguities of life. Security and stability lie in preserving the belief (taught by their parents, usually) that there is no such thing as luck. If good things have happened to them, TKIAs believe it is because they have earned them, through their own determination and effort.

If something they try goes wrong, it can be devastating to a TKIA and his or her sense of self-confidence and control. For others, making a mistake is just human, and admitting a mistake is merely humbling. For TKIAs, the idea of making mistakes is impermissible in their carefully constructed world view, and admitting a mistake would be humiliating and emotionally overwhelming. Unlike Type III chronic complainers and no-people, whose locus of control over their lives is totally outside of themselves, TKIAs see control of their lives residing entirely within, in their unquestionably superior knowledge. Since they are convinced that others have nothing relevant to offer, they may treat others as if they were irrelevant. It is easy to understand why others respond to the TKIA's unjust, condescending treatment with anger, frequently expressed either in open hostility or in some of subtler, passive-aggressive ways.

## DEALING WITH TKIAS

Understanding the motivation behind TKIA behavior may provide a key to changing our own emotional and behavioral responses to them, instead of merely reacting. TKIAs are driven by a compulsive need for control in a world that is actually, for the most part, out of their control. Each time they succeed in achieving some goal, their vision of themselves as in-charge and self-directed is reinforced. However, while they appear to act out of a position of power and certainty, they are constantly but unconsciously engaged in an internal struggle to maintain their fragile sense of safety and security. The goal in dealing with them is not to destroy this tenuous structure and the TKIA with it. You cannot reasonably expect to change the TKIAs' behavior (this only *they* can do). If you think of your interactions with people as "win-or-lose" battles, everyone will eventually lose, regardless of who comes out on top. What can you do? You can begin looking at your relationships with TKIAs from a different frame of reference. This means changing your *own responses* to them and seeking to get your *own needs* met. It means striving in your interactions with TKIAs to *have your own contributions and worth acknowledged* and affirmed.

Since TKIAs can be counted on to find the weaknesses in any opinions other than their own, it is wise not to feed them ammunition that can be used against you. If you want this person to accept what you have to offer, you should *be sure and be prepared ahead of time*. You need to know what you are talking about and know the flaws in your own opinions. You should resolve to make your interaction to be a true exchange of ideas, not two egos lobbing artillery shells across enemy lines! Having people listen and accept as truth what a TKIA says is exactly what he or she thrives on. This is not the time for a spontaneous philosophical discussion of the ambiguities and uncertainties of a situation, much as that may be your preferred style. It is, however, the perfect time to *repeat back virtually everything you hear*, in complete detail. To hear one's own ideas and opinions *quoted* by someone else is music to TKIAs' ears! If you don't literally repeat what they say, they will probably do it themselves in greater detail. So you should listen carefully. If a TKIA can see that you are really listening, that you acknowledge and respect his or her knowledge, you are far less likely to be seen as a threat. Also, the fact that you have taken the time and effort to anticipate his or her interests, and think through his or her potential objections, will further reduce the perceived differences between the TKIA and us.

When you feel that you have the TKIA's attention, you can begin to *discuss your ideas in a respectful, non-competitive way*. The

TKIA does not want to hear another know-it-all. So you should use tentative words, such as "maybe," "perhaps," and "I'm not sure about this, but. . . ." Also, using inclusive pronouns such as "we," "us," and "our," instead of "I" and "you," will automatically place you and the TKIA on the same team in a cooperative, rather than competitive mode. *Putting your statement or objection in the form of a question* is also a more indirect way of getting the TKIA to listen and weigh its merits. For example, "What if we were to try _____ next time?" Often, the TKIA will overcome the stumbling blocks just by talking it through with you. But first, you have to make it safe for the TKIA to listen and respond nondefensively.

Depending on how much time and energy you feel it is worth, you can *build an informal mentoring relationship* with the TKIA by letting the person know how much you respect and wish to learn from his or her knowledge. When dealing with TKIAs, it is important to remember that they really *are* intelligent, experienced, and knowledgeable people, and that they really want to be appreciated for it. You may have to defer to their superior attitude, even let them take credit for your successful idea, at first. But the more you keep applying the communication suggestions outlined above, the more in control of the interaction you will be, and the more you can draw TKIAs into an alliance with you.

TKIAs are highly task-oriented, rather aggressive, and want to get things done—their way. By building a positive relationship with them, learning from them, and getting them to see that their way and yours are not all that different, you will be seen as less and less of a threat and more and more of a partner. By being persistent in your behavior changes with them, you may eventually even have TKIAs *asking* you for your ideas before you offer them.

# THE WOULD-BE EXPERT

I couldn't help but overhear that lady asking you about removing those stains from her carpet. I just read an article that said you should use ginger ale on it. I'm sure that that would work. . . .

Bogus *experts* are relatively easy to distinguish from true experts. Their reputation often precedes them in the form of warnings from people who have made the mistake of taking their advice seriously, with disastrous results. Would-Be Know-It-Alls (WBKIAs) are different from TKIAs in several important ways. First, they are not experts at all, except at being able to fool some people (for awhile) into believing that they know something. While TKIAs and WBKIAs both tend to be actively assertive or aggressive, the WBKIA is people-oriented (Type I) rather than task-oriented. They want the *attention* of others, not appreciation for their knowledge, which tends to be a random collection of bits of information and pieces of misinformation, often presented in a misleading but entertaining way. Unlike the Type II TKIA, who will expound on a pet idea repeatedly in great detail, without regard to effect on the listener, the primary intent of Type I WBKIAs is to get the listener's attention and keep it focused on the WBKIA, regardless of the accuracy and worth of the ideas.

WBKIAs' style of speaking is more distinguished by its process than its content, the idea being to capture and hold the listener's attention with the speed and energy of their message, and hope that the listener will *buy* the ideas on the strength of the presentation. Uninitiated listeners who allow themselves to fall under a WBKIA's spell often discover later, much to their chagrin, that they have "bought a lemon." Once burned, they learn to steer clear of the WBKIA and his or her bad ideas. When the situation requires that they interact with this person, they remember what happened before and wish they could simply tell the WBKIA to shut up. Indeed, while WBKIAs can have other admirable qualities and can serve useful functions, they also have the potential to waste other people's time and resources, leaving them feeling betrayed and suspicious. The difficult behavior of WBKIAs often turns out to be self-defeating. That is, rather than getting the attention they want and need, their victims learn to reject and ignore what they have to say.

## HOW DID THE WBKIA GET THIS WAY?

If we quickly peruse some of the many celebrity biographies available in our libraries, or watch a number of television interviews with famous entertainers, a common thread appears. Somewhere in their formative years some of these people were shown or told by people who were powerful and important to them that they (the WBKIAs) were *not* important. They have maintained this belief into adulthood. To make up for these early and continuing blows to their self-esteem, WBKIAs develop a constant craving for the attention of other people and behave in the ways described above to get it. For many people, the ability to entertain others has been not only a way to make a good living but also a means of overcoming and changing their early beliefs in their own unworthiness. Both they and their audiences reap the benefits. However, while they are usually likeable Type I people, most WBKIAs do not become professional entertainers. Instead, they substitute style for the substance they lack, often speaking with great authority and very little information. They perform their attention-getting act in inappropriate situations, where the focus needs to be on the problem to be solved, not on the Would-Be Know-It-All.

## DEALING WITH WBKIAS

As with every other type of difficult person we have discussed, the goal in dealing with the Type I, Would-Be Know-It-All, is to tailor your response to his or her needs and intentions while keeping your own goals in the forefront. *WBKIAs need the attention, respect, and admiration of others.* Your goal with them, again, is not to attempt to change them, and their behavior, but to present your objections and alternatives to their bad ideas. However, the way to do this is not to put the WBKIA on the defensive. To attack the WBKIA and his or her ideas directly, implying that the person is either lying or incompetent, would be destructive, both to the WBKIA and to group morale. Often WBKIAs really think they know what they are talking about, and that what they are saying is the truth. You want them to recognize that they are missing important information, without making them lose face in an open confrontation. In fact, the direct approach will probably result in one of two more undesirable outcomes:

1. The WBKIA will be forced to defend his or her faulty ideas by repeating them over and over (which is a subtle method of reinforcing them), or
2. While you may see through the WBKIA's arguments, others may not and may even rise to the WBKIA's defense (also a form of reinforcement).

Therefore, openly confronting the WBKIA is the worst thing you can do!

As with the True Know-It-Alls, *the indirect approach* works best with Would-Be Know-It-Alls. This means giving the WBKIA your attention (which he or she craves), and responding by repeating back to the person what he or she has said (which keeps the WBKIA from repeating and reinforcing himself or herself). *Ask questions that call for WBKIAs to be specific.* This helps them to reveal fully the true extent of their knowledge on the subject, which is probably very little. When you know that they have no more information to offer, you should not embarrass them by pressing for more. Rather, you can use what they have said as a springboard for presenting your ideas and for clarifying, correcting, and expanding on the information presented by the WBKIA and others. For example, say something like, "I'm really glad you brought this up, Greg, because it's really important that we talk about this thoroughly before we make a decision." Then, using "I" language, *shift the other listeners' attention to yourself*. Tell the WBKIA and others what you think they need to know. Again, as with any presentation of information, you need to be prepared with accurate information (having the facts in writing adds to their power), and to anticipate the potential doubts and concerns of others. But more importantly, by giving a WBKIA respectful attention and recognition, you have fulfilled the person's deepest need and allowed him or her to save face. You can now safely shift the focus to a thorough discussion of the problem or task at hand.

**A word of caution:** The techniques described above will help you to cope in individual encounters with Would-Be Know-It-Alls by allowing both of you to fulfill needs and goals. However, they are merely short-term solutions to immediate difficult situations. They do not address the long-term problems presented by WBKIAs, namely, their constant reliance on slick presentation to get attention and hide their lack of substantive knowledge. To address this problem will require a long-term commitment on your part to helping the WBKIAs break this negative habit. You must decide whether it is worth the time and effort on your part. If you do resolve to pursue a long-term course of action, you may need to confront squarely your own negative feelings about the WBKIA and acknowledge the ways in which they can bias your thinking about them. For example, if you have been the unfortunate victim of one of these people, you may dislike him or her intensely, and your dislike may grow more intense with each encounter. Your dislike of his or her interpersonal style may get generalized to the point that it causes you to unfairly dismiss *everything* he or she says as irrelevant, regardless of its validity.

The way to turn this behavioral cycle around is to *shift your focus from the negative to the positive*. In other words, you should begin by trying to catch the WBKIA doing or saying something right, and giving him or her credit for it. If you try to ignore everything a WBKIA says and does, including the things that are useful and valid, the WBKIA will simply try harder to get your attention by increasing his or her annoying (and irrelevant) attention-getting behaviors. However, if you consistently pay attention and openly and verbally *acknowledge the things you like and value*, the WBKIA will eventually get the message that these are the kinds of things he or she will have to produce to get your attention.

# References

1.  Robert M. Bramsom, *Coping With Difficult People*. (New York: Ballantine Books, 1981), 93-95.

# 11 THE NON-TRADITIONAL CLIENT

At 8:45 every morning seven patrons stand near the main entrance to the city library to await its opening. When the doors are unlocked, these patrons head directly to the restrooms, where they shave, or wash up. Then they proceed to the magazine and newspaper areas, where they occupy the upholstered sofas and chairs for most of the day, occasionally reading but mostly just sitting, staring into space, chatting with each other, or sleeping until the library closes, and it's time to head back to the night shelter or the street. . . .

In a 1989 article, Herbert S. White notes that, in the last several decades, there has been a shift in the general mission of American library service to a "mindset that looks at librarianship as a social service rather than as a educational or informational profession."[1] White's article is a relatively recent appraisal of an issue that has a long history of controversy within the field of library service. In simple terms, the issue revolves around the question: Whom shall the library serve and how? Shall it serve only those people whose education, socioeconomic status, and other demographic characteristics place them in the economic and social mainstream of the community, those who seek the educational and informational services that librarians and libraries are traditionally equipped to provide (the so-called "information rich")? Or shall its limited staff time and resources be stretched and refocused to serve people who, for lack of education, status, and mobility or for other reasons, are more marginal to mainstream society, those who do not normally seek the library's traditional services, or who are unable to make use of these services as traditionally provided (the "information poor")?

This question has been rehashed time and time again, with no general resolution within the profession as a whole. On the other hand, it has been observed that some libraries and library staff (both professional and support staff) seem to have come to grips with this issue and resolved it for themselves. They appear to have reframed the question and moved beyond it, committing their resources to serving not only the patrons who are most prepared to use the library as a traditional institution but also those who are least prepared with the fewest resources. Rather than restating their powerlessness to address major social problems, these library staff have evidently been successful at *empowering themselves* to offer innovative, multi-phased programs, staff training, and other strategies designed to serve the nontraditional client (e.g., the poor; the very young; the elderly; the homeless; the unemployed or underemployed; the illiterate; those who are physically, mentally, emotionally, educationally, culturally or otherwise disabled; the dysfunctional; and the powerless).

The library people who choose to serve library clienteles in all their manifestations must be able to communicate with large numbers of diverse individuals and groups, many of whom are quite dissimilar to the people staffing the public service desks. Depending upon a staff member's philosophy of service and perception of a patron's similarity to oneself, he or she may experience a wide range of ease or frustration in communicating and providing service. Public service staff members often experience communication problems even when dealing with their traditional or *normal* library users.

Basic questions that must be asked are both philosophical and practical in nature: What principles, values, and attitudes motivate and sustain library staff who attempt to serve the needs of individuals and groups that are traditionally unserved or underserved by libraries? How do library people manage communication and service to these sectors of society, many of whom represent much wider social problems than the library alone can resolve? What barriers (including values, attitudes, policies, and skill deficiencies) interfere with their ability to communicate and provide service to these (or for that matter, any) individuals and groups? And how do libraries and library people overcome barriers to communication and service (particularly in concert with other community agencies)? In an age and pluralistic society that is increasingly dependent on information for survival, and in a time of increasing polarization of American society between rich and poor and between the "information rich" and the "information poor," answers to these and other such questions require thoughtful research, from which basic theories and philosophies can evolve about how we might effectively serve everyone in the library's community regardless of status.

# ALL THE LONELY PEOPLE

These broad, sweeping questions are far beyond the scope of this book to answer. However, as noted earlier, the nontraditional client groups enumerated above are frequently cited in connection with the phrase problem patron.[2] Therefore, it may be helpful to explore selected examples of these nontraditional groups (i.e., the homeless poor and the "latchkey" child) in order to better understand the wider context of the difficult behaviors they bring to the library, as well as some basic ideas for meeting their needs more effectively. Selected reading lists for further study of each group in the context of library service may be found in Appendix B.

## WHO ARE THE HOMELESS POOR?

Americans who are homeless are becoming increasingly visible on streets and in public parks and buildings across the country. By the beginning of the 1990s, popular media estimates of the number of homeless men, women, and children ranged as high as three million.[3]

Research has identified a number of factors that contribute to the rising incidence of homelessness in the United States. While it might seem an oversimplification (or circular logic) to attribute this phenomenon to a lack of sufficient income to prevent extreme poverty, the fact is that *people are homeless largely because they cannot afford to pay for their housing, food, and other needs.* One important variable has been the decline in employment opportunities for low-skilled or unskilled workers. The need for an increasingly educated workforce, along with increased use of automation and other sophisticated technology, has virtually eliminated demand for the kinds of casual labor that once sustained the skid-row resident of a few decades ago.

In many American cities' "flop houses" and other low-rent housing for single people has given way to demolition, gentrification, or conversion to high-priced condominium dwellings for a higher class of city-dweller. Discrimination along racial and ethnic lines continues to limit employment opportunities of minorities. Chronic poverty over several generations is significantly associated with the incidence of crime, violence, abuse (including drugs and alcohol), and dysfunction in individuals and among families, neighborhoods, and larger societal groups. Extended economic recession, plus the failure of social welfare programs to keep up with inflation and the reduced supply of low-cost housing, has led to a steady increase in the proportion of the American population who are down and out—under the poverty line and literally on the street. Contrary to the stereotype of the drunken vagrant, it is now single parents, mostly mothers, with young children who comprise the fastest growing segment of the homeless population,[4] and who are most at risk of getting caught in a lifelong downward spiral of poverty and helplessness.

In addition, there has been much discussion in the literature on "deinstitutionalization" and how it has changed both the reality and our perceptions of street people. It is generally believed that at least one-third of homeless persons are mentally ill. Thirty-five to forty percent suffer from alcohol or other substance abuse.[5] A few decades ago, individuals with physical, mental, or behavioral disabilities that prevented them from earning a living or caring for themselves were likely to be either cared for privately or institutionalized. Community mental health concepts and legislation of the 1960s are associated with the deinstitutionalization of a large number of individuals who eventually became homeless. However, there is also an increasing number of homeless people who have never been institutionalized in total-care facilities but who might have been a generation or more ago. These people tend to be among the poorest of the poor, people whose families and resources cannot bear the overwhelming cost of caring for one's own. This cost is not only financial but personal and social as well. The social and personal factors related to homelessness will be explored in further detail next.

# RESEARCH ON HOMELESSNESS

In a study of the homeless in Chicago, sociologists Peter H. Rossi and James D. Wright described homelessness as:

> a manifestation of extreme poverty that occurs among disabled and isolated people. . . . a heterogeneous mixture of chronic long-term and transitory short-term homelessness. . . . Despite their demographic mix, [the homeless] are relatively homogeneous in at least three critical respects: (1) they are extremely poor; (2) they exhibit high levels of physical, mental, and social disabilities; (3) they display high levels of social isolation, with extremely weak or nonexistent ties to others. . . . Surprisingly few were on public welfare. . . . [They had been] unemployed much longer than they had been homeless, by about three years. . . . This finding suggests that many unemployed single persons are helped out by their families and friends for relatively long periods, but that the patience, forbearance, or resources of these benefactors eventually run out, with literal homelessness resulting.[7]

The social isolation of the homeless, exacerbated in a vicious circle by their disabilities, makes the probability of change in their status highly unlikely. Few of these individuals described by Rossi and Wright were able to maintain regular contact with friends and family members, and only nine percent were members of households, a group almost exclusively comprised of homeless women and their children. As a result, the homeless are denied the normal "buffering effects of extended kin or friendship networks, making them especially vulnerable to the ups and downs of fortune caused by changes in employment and in physical or mental health." Regarding the latter, Rossi and Wright go on to say that, in their data, one or more disabling conditions were reported by four out of five (82 percent) of their sample. The homeless reported that they:

1. were in fair or poor health;
2. had been in a mental hospital;
3. had been in a detoxification unit;
4. had received clinically high scores on one of the psychiatric morbidity scales; and/or
5. had been sentenced by a court.[7]

While it is obvious that homelessness is related to extreme poverty, it is also true that there are many extremely poor people who are *not* homeless. Matthew W. Stagner and Harold A. Richman's study of welfare recipients, also conducted in Chicago, reports that people who were eligible for general assistance (GA) payments for single people closely resembled the homeless: Most were male, black, and unmarried, although they were slightly younger (average age 34 compared with age 40 for the homeless). However, there were some important and significant differences. The GA recipients:

1. were much more likely (about 80 percent) to be either living with or getting financial help from family and friends;
2. were much less likely to be physically disabled so as to be unemployable (only 9 percent) or to have been in mental hospitals (1 percent); and
3. had been, on the average, unemployed for a much shorter period of time (19 months as opposed to three years for the homeless).[8]

## LACK OF SOCIAL NETWORKS
While many of the non-homeless poor in the study were at great risk, the single most conspicuous factor apparently protecting

them from homelessness was their *social networks*. Unfortunately, the family and friends of extremely poor people are very likely to be poor themselves. While the desire to help may be there, the ability to share one's resources with another adult for indefinite periods of time is probably not. This reality, when complicated by frequent and serious behavioral problems on the part of the individual in question, contributes to deterioration of the bonds of attachment and support, resulting in eventual rejection and homelessness.

As Rossi and Wright conclude, the homeless poor are *socially isolated adults* who have been unable, by reason of physical or mental disability, or rejection by family and friends, to benefit from the supportive and defensive structures such networks provide. Ironically, the political climate of the 1980s saw both a dramatic increase in the incidence of homelessness and a dramatic decline in social welfare programs targeted at the poorest of the poor.[9]

With limited shelter facilities and nowhere else to go, the homeless poor are appearing with increasing frequency in libraries. Often the library is the only public building in the town that does not require the visitor to have a purpose in being there. Ironically, the commitment of many libraries to provide welcoming, comfortable, quiet facilities for their browsers has made them highly attractive places for many street people to spend their idle hours. What is problematic for library staff and other patrons is *not* the fact that they are homeless. On the contrary, libraries and individual library staff who have made a special commitment to provide the poor and homeless members of their communities with *traditional* library services have often frequently played an important role in ensuring the people's right to know, empowering them and changing lives. A 1993 American Library Association fact sheet included such examples as:

> . . . the homeless man in Boston who spent all his time in the library studying how to become a writer. Today he is a published, self-supporting freelance journalist. . . . [and] the little girl who spent all her free time in an East Toledo branch library, reading to escape from an impoverished home and the burden of caring for her mentally ill mother. Today Gloria Steinem, the well known author and feminist, says: "I am entirely a product of libraries. You have made me what I am today."[10]

In addition, many libraries have instituted innovative *nontraditional* programs (in cooperation with other community service agencies) to serve the poor and homeless, including, for example "street cards" listing food banks, shelters, health and legal services, and welfare and employment opportunities (Baltimore County, MD); referral services to agencies that help the poor and homeless (San Diego, Memphis/Shelby County, TN, and Cumberland County,NC); borrower's cards for people without permanent addresses (San Francisco and Philadelphia); community rooms in the library specifically for use by the homeless (Haverill, MA); and book collections, literacy instruction, and story hours in shelters and homeless centers (New York, Tulsa City-County, OK, and Greensboro, NC).[11]

Rather, the complaints about the homeless poor in the library have more to do with personal hygiene and/or disturbing behavior (for example, the highly publicized case involving Richard Kreimer and the Morristown Public Library). Objections to street people range from offensive body odors, to bathing in the library restrooms, to alcohol or drug abuse, to active hallucination, to following and staring at other people, to "flashing," loud talking, cursing, and yelling, all the way to illegal, threatening, dangerous, and destructive acts. Most of these problems are symptomatic of the multiple physical, mental and social disabilities and isolation that dictate the everyday lives of many homeless poor people and mark them as one of the groups most frequently, and euphemistically, identified as problem patrons.

# ALL THE LONELY (YOUNG) PEOPLE

Almost every day at 3:00 p.m., ten-year-old Tracy enters the library with her little sister Ellen, who is six. Tracy and Ellen remain at the library until 8 o'clock, when their mother comes to pick them up at the end of her work shift. During their hours at the library, Tracy plays with Ellen and sometimes reads to her. Mostly, though, she talks with her friends from school, who are there working on homework assignments or just hanging out. Ellen often wanders about the library, stopping to chat with the "lady at the desk," who sometimes lets her *help*. Both girls are generally well-behaved, although their frequent runny noses and untidy appearance are causes for concern for some staff members and regular patrons. Their mother seems to be a gentle, tired-looking woman. She smiles but rarely says more than hello to anyone at the library.

Throughout most of the history of western civilization, libraries existed for adults, scholars in particular, and most definitely were *not* intended to be used by children. It is only in this century, particularly the latter half, that library services for young people have begun to receive the enthusiasm and attention that they deserve. Children depend on adults to meet their basic physical, emotional, and spiritual needs. Because of the dependency needs that characterize the various stages of their development and growth, young people have always been vulnerable to behavioral problems arising out of abandonment and neglect.

## LATCHKEY CHILDREN

The phenomenon of the latchkey child has received a great deal of attention in library professional literature. Lynette Long and Thomas Long, in their *Handbook for Latchkey Children and Their Parents*, defined latchkey children as, "Children who are regularly left during some part of the day to supervise themselves, whether during the time they use group recreation programs, play in the street, stay home alone, join a gang, or for whom child care arrangements are so loosely made that they are virtually ineffective."[12] Whether they are left completely alone or in charge of other children, the important concept in this definition is the fact that they are left *without adult supervision* on a *regular* basis.

The millions of American latchkey children represent a cross-section of American society, including all economic levels, racial, ethnic, and religious segments of the population. The term latchkey refers to stereotypical children of school age who wear or carry their own house keys with them in order to let themselves in after school, and before their parents arrive home from work. Indeed, families with single parents (usually mothers), or with both parents working (out of choice or necessity), are the overwhelming norm in the 1990s. Combine this fact with the noticeable shortage of adequate, affordable daycare, and the rising numbers of homeless children, and we can reasonably conclude that most American children, at some point in their young lives, will be left at least some hours of the day to care for themselves.

As with the homeless, a great deal of research has been, and still remains to be, conducted on the values, needs, and attitudes of latchkey children and their parents. The problems associated with leaving children in self-care are skillfully described by Frances Dowd in her highly recommended book *Latchkey Children in the Library and Community*.[13] They include alcohol and drug use, unsupervised watching of controversial television programs, and sexual experimentation, as well as a variety of health, safety, and educational issues. For many parents, the library offers a safe, visible, quiet, and convenient alternative to the trouble their children could get into on the street or in the house. Some children choose to spend their after-school hours at the library, but many do not. They are there because they have been instructed to be there, but often without any further expectation or instruction. For many of the library staff members interviewed by Dowd, dealing with the collective behavior of large numbers of energetic (and often hungry) children, and the attitudes of their parents, is problematic. They can cite numerous examples of inappropriate behavior, such as running, fighting, moving of furniture, excessive noise, even inadvertent or intentional destruction of property. Parents who are late picking up their children at closing time also create safety and possibly legal problems for some staff members.

## Opportunity to Serve

For others, however, the presence of latchkey children in the library is seen as an opportunity to reach out and serve a somewhat captive audience of future adult library users.[14] (Again, the way one basically views a problem often is the problem.) In her book, Dowd recommends a multi-faceted *cooperative* community approach for meeting the needs of latchkey children, involving not only the library but the schools, recreation centers, institutions of higher education, businesses, and local, state, and federal governments. Indeed, in the past decade, numerous school and public libraries, in particular, have responded to this nontraditional group of young library visitors by adopting policies, programs, materials, and services, as well as setting aside separate areas of the library building, to focus on the developmental, educational, and recreational needs of unattended children.

For example, in addition to reading and audiovisual materials, library personnel at the Weber County Public Library provided arts and crafts materials and created workbooks for children to use in the library after school. Staff at the Brooklyn Public Library will hold books at the circulation desk for children who cannot take them home. Other libraries offer a self-care or homework hotline for children to call, and regularly include the discussions of the needs of this group in staff training and development sessions.[15]

# WHAT CAN THE LIBRARY DO?

Salter and Salter, Dowd, and many other researchers and writers emphasize the importance of strong but flexible library policies and procedures that enable library staff to uphold the rights of all people, regardless of status, to access and use the library's resources and materials, while ensuring the safety of library users and staff along with the protection of the library's resources and facility. In 1993, the American Library Association's Intellectual Freedom Committee issued its *Guidelines for the Development of Policies and Procedures Regarding User Behavior and Library Usage*.[16] These guidelines (see Appendix C) thoughtfully address the need for fairness, reason, and common sense in policies and procedures that must balance freedom of expression with certain restrictions on behavior.

The guidelines also strongly recommend that libraries make a concerted effort to build coalitions between themselves and other agencies and caregivers in the community so that a cooperative, coordinated approach to these larger societal problems is possible. Part of the problem for many libraries is that staff often feel that they are taken for granted, left alone to deal with the problem behaviors of individuals who come to the library largely because they have been forsaken by their families and other social institutions. By researching such issues as homelessness and latchkey children, for example, and by educating and training themselves and others about issues and appropriate strategies, library staff contribute to the achievement of the library's mission to inform. By initiating cooperative training and community action activities with other public and private sector organizations, libraries stand a much better chance of success in actually ameliorating some of the behavioral problems exacerbated by poverty and neglect. One thing is certain, the library *cannot* do it alone.

## WHAT CAN THE INDIVIDUAL STAFF MEMBER DO?

One could make a strong case that homelessness, for example, is a societal problem calling for societal solutions on a large scale (e.g., welfare reform and other social legislation). However, it is also true that individuals can make a difference on a smaller scale by acknowledging that the problem of homelessness exists in their communities and by taking responsibility for their own responses to it when it impacts their sphere of influence, no matter how large or small. For example, the formerly homeless Boston man who is now a self-supporting freelance writer attributed much of his progress to the supportive kindness and service provided to him by individual library staff members. Pat Woodrum, director of the Tulsa City-County Library System, invited representatives of the various community service agencies to a meeting in order to focus on the problems of the homeless poor in her area. As a result, Tulsa established a day center providing safety, food, clothing, medical care, counseling, reading material, and companionship for street people.[17]

The first steps are *awareness and understanding*.

Next is a renewed *commitment to uphold the legal and human rights and intellectual freedom and access of all* members of one's community by adopting and adhering to policies and programs that extend the library's services with fairness to everyone.

Finally, we can all take *personal responsibility to treat library patrons, traditional or nontraditional, with assertiveness, compassion, and respect*, by consistently applying the basic principles of effective communication described in this book.

As the ancient Chinese curse (or blessing) says, "May you live in interesting times." We do. Let us learn and enjoy.

# References

1. Herbert S. White, "Send These, the Homeless, Tempest-Tost to Me," *Library Journal*, Vol. 114 (February 15, 1989), pp. 146-147.
2. An excellent guide to the origins, types and historical treatments of mental illness and emotional disturbance, plus steps for preparing for and handling encounters with the troublesome behaviors that are often symptomatic of them, may be found in Charles A. Salter and Jeffrey A. Salter's *On the Frontlines: Coping with the Library's Problem Patron* (Englewood, CO: Libraries Unlimited, 1988). In addition, the authors provide 24 case studies for analysis and discussion by library staff. Included are patron behaviors ranging from the harmless and annoying behavior to the dangerous and criminal. Salter and Salter suggest training methods and potential sources of community help.

   Another valuable training resource is Bruce A. Shuman's *River Bend Revisited: The Problem Patron in the Library* (Phoenix, AZ: Oryx Press, 1984). Following the format of Shuman's earlier work, *The River Bend Casebook: Problems in Public Library Service* (Phoenix, AZ: Oryx Press, 1981), this volume contains over three dozen extensive case studies dealing with various problem behaviors of library patrons, both adults and young people. Situations range from emergencies and hazards to nuisances, each followed by questions for discussion and lists of additional resources.
3. Lisa Orr, *The Homeless* (San Diego, CA: Greenhaven Press, 1990), p. 17.

4. Amy S. Wells, "Educating Homeless Children," *Education Digest*, Vol. 55 (April 1990), p. 30.

5. Albert Gore, Jr., "Public Policy and the Homeless," *American Psychologist*, Vol. 45 (August 1990), p. 960.

6. Peter H. Rossi and James D. Wright, "The Determinants of Homelessness," *Health Affairs*, Vol. 6 (Spring 1987), pp. 19-21.

7. Ibid., 24.

8. M. Stagner and H. Richman, *General Assistance Families* (Chicago: National Opinion Research Center, 1985).

9. Rossi and Wright, op. cit., p. 30.

10. "Fact Sheet: Libraries Change Lives," Public Information Office, American Library Association, March 1993, p. 1.

11. "Fact Sheet: America's Libraries and the Homeless," Public Information Office, American Library Association, December 1991, pp. 1-2.

12. L. Long and T. Long, *Handbook for Latchkey Children and Their Parents* (New York: Arbor House, 1983).

13. Frances Smardo Dowd, *Latchkey Children in the Library and Community: Issues, Strategies and Programs* (Phoenix, AZ: Oryx Press, 1991), passim. Smardo's book is also outstanding for its lists of recommended print and audiovisual resources for both adults and children.

14. Ibid.

15. Ibid., 164-169.

16. American Library Association, Committee on Intellectual Freedom, *Guidelines for the Development of Policies and Procedures Regarding User Behavior and Library Usage.* (Chicago: American Library Association, January 24, 1993).

Many libraries are in the process of developing, or have already adopted, policies that ensure access to information and services for all members of the community, along with procedures for dealing with user behavior problems. These policies and procedures then become part of the foundation of staff training and development related to customer services.

State and national library associations are an excellent source of support for the development of these types of policies and procedures. The American Library Association's Office of Intellectual Freedom (50 E. Huron Street, Chicago, IL 60611) offers continuing education, handbooks, newsletters, and other materials to guide library staffs in compiling their own policy statements. ALA resources include the "Library Bill of Rights" (and interpretive statements), the "Statement on Professional Ethics," and the recently approved "Guidelines for the Development of Policies Regarding User Behavior and Library Usage." The various ALA divisions and roundtables are also outstanding sources of guidance and information having to do with policies and services to people of various age-levels and specific needs.

17. "Fact Sheet: America's Libraries and the Homeless," p. 2.

# 12 PREPARING STAFF TO DEAL WITH DIFFICULT CUSTOMERS

Most libraries allocate the largest proportion of their operating budgets to human resources, and assign high value to the quality of public service activities. The backbone of every library's mission in its community is the creation of opportunities for lifelong learning and effective service. The library's ability to carry out its mission rests with the abilities of its staff to communicate and handle interactions with users and each other, especially the difficult situations, effectively and in a professional manner.

However, decades of experience and research have shown us that people who work in libraries and other service-oriented agencies were neither born with highly effective communication and conflict-resolution skills, nor likely to have developed these kinds of skills in the formal education programs established to prepare them for library occupations. Preparation of library staff to deal effectively with all kinds of people, difficult or not, requires ongoing continuing education, training, and staff development.

## THE WHYS AND HOWS OF GOOD TRAINING

Effective training requires effective communication and presentation skills on the part of well-selected trainers, skills that result in positive changes in staff attitudes, understanding, competency, and behavior. Most library people want to be competent and effective in what they do. They want to serve their customers well. Good training inspires individual staff members to *want* to change and grow, in order to serve their customers better. But good training cannot happen without the cooperation and support of everyone—the managers, the trainers, and the participants themselves. And trainees' newly acquired concepts and skills cannot become lifelong habits without the opportunity and support of the library and each other for applying newly-learned concepts and skills to real situations on the job.

It is vital to the success of any training or staff development effort that new knowledge and skill be recognized as having value in the corporate culture. Staff members need to see that the changes they are being asked to make are relevant to their success in

**139**

building work competency and serving the library's patrons or customers effectively, especially those people who present them with the greatest interpersonal challenges.

Managers can reinforce the value and importance of positive behavioral change in dealing with difficult customers in a number of ways:

1. By making participation in customer serving training part of every staff member's list of duties and responsibilities.
2. By consulting with each individual to determine specific training needs and styles of learning, develop a flexible training plan, outline expectations of change, help to find good trainers, and arrange appropriate individual or group training experiences.
3. By allocating sufficient funds and staff time to allow preparation for, participation in, and followup on training experiences.
4. By providing opportunities, feedback, and rewards for application of knowledge and skills learned through training.

Good trainers must be good communicators who understand the needs and goals of staff members and how these relate to the mission and needs of the library as an organization. They must possess, not only expertise, but good sense and goodwill. They should be able to model effective ways of solving problems and resolving conflict. They know that people are more likely to remember and *own* changes in their behavior if they have the opportunity to decide what changes need to be made. They know the value of group effort in discovery and support of effective solutions to problems. They know that the development of interpersonal communication skills is not simply an intellectual pursuit; it requires opportunities for staff to learn through reality-based experiential exercises and practice in an environment characterized by safety and mutual support. They also know that real change is evolutionary and takes time.

Library staff members who regularly interact with other people in the course of their everyday duties must have the ability to relate and work with others in ways that promote cooperation, so that the needs of clients are addressed and fulfilled productively. It is not enough for library staff members to know all about library materials, systems, processes, policies, and procedures. They must be able to communicate their understanding of these technical aspects of their jobs in such a way that the individual who needs the library's resources is helped in some way. The goal is to help people make effective use of these resources, both material and human, to gain knowledge, solve a problem, or accomplish a task.

Depending on the time available and the objectives and abilities of users, the helping process can involve interpersonal skills that range from simple information-giving to bibliographic instruction, from advising to mediation, from supervision to negotiation, to support and counseling. Different skills are appropriate to different situations and clients, as demonstrated in other chapters of this book.

One recurring theme in our discussion of communication and difficult behavior has been the concept of personal power and control. Whenever one person approaches another for help, there is a delicate shift in the balance of power between them. Library staff need to understand that, along with the helping role, they have the power to influence the thinking, feelings, and behavior of those they serve, and a corresponding responsibility to use and share that power in a professional manner—that is, effectively and wisely—in partnership with, and for the benefit of, the people they serve. In a sense, this means library staff need the ability and have the responsibility to empower the people they are there to serve in the library.

# THE PHILOSOPHY AND PRACTICE OF EMPOWERMENT

If empowerment of one's clients and associates is the ultimate purpose of library service, the means by which library staff share personal power and build partnerships with others are person-centered. Carl Rogers, founder of the "client-centered" approach to personal growth, described the primary characteristics of empowering people in terms of self-awareness, authenticity, honesty, openness, nonjudgmental acceptance of others as persons, and empathy.[1] People who develop and base their daily relationships and interactions with others on the basis of these personal principles enable themselves and others to

1. feel more confident,
2. function more effectively,
3. have a greater sense of competence and autonomy,

4. understand each other more empathically,
5. accept each other more openly, and
6. deal with problems and difficulties more serenely and philosophically.

We empower others when we value, trust, and respect people as individuals and celebrate their abilities. In terms of library service, empowerment translates into using communication to help people find out what they want and need, then providing them with the information, instruction, encouragement, and feedback necessary to get what they want and need. It means helping people to define their own objectives and goals, generate strategies, and take action to reach those goals and objectives. It means providing opportunities for people to take risks, make mistakes, earn recognition, and learn and grow in an environment of security and acceptance.

By learning and developing proficiency in the skills described in this book (communication, assertiveness, cooperation, conflict-resolution, and decision-making), and by sharing them, library staff can empower themselves and empower their clients, co-workers, family and friends, as well as their difficult customers.

# THE CHALLENGE TO MANAGEMENT

If libraries are to be successful in achieving the ideal of empowerment through service, the importance of a knowledgeable staff, trained in the very skills that empower people to take control of their own needs, problems, and life situations to the fullest possible extent, cannot be overstated. Investment in the library's human resources includes a solid continuing education and training program. Libraries need people who can recognize and mobilize their own powers and abilities to make a difference in their clients and their communities. They need people who can see problems as challenges, and who can make decisions that matter. For library staff to be effective, they must be able to find meaning in their work while cultivating self-esteem and trust. They should have opportunities to learn, communicate openly, set their own priorities, seek help and get support from others, contribute their own ideas and energy to the process, and share in its results.

Managers and governing authorities of all libraries would do well, therefore, to make staff development and training in customer service and communication a long-term, high priority in terms of both time and expenditure, along with the establishment and regular review of service policies and procedures. The following outline for the development of policies, procedures, and staff training in customer service is offered as suggested structure for use by those who are responsible for library services or the development of library staff.

I. Developing Policy
   A. Gathering background information
   B. Following recommended guidelines
   C. Writing the policy statement
   D. Securing official approval
   E. Disseminating the policy

II. Developing Procedures
   A. Compiling factual information (directories of relevant individuals, social service agencies, government/ law enforcement agencies, etc.)
   B. Defining specific duties, responsibilities, authority of individuals and groups, in the library and in the community.
   C. Writing step-by-step procedures for handling routine customer service and problems

III. Developing Training
   A. Group and individual activities
     1. Assessing needs
     2. Determining objectives
     3. Designing and presenting activities
     4. Promoting activities
     5. Evaluating activities and their effectiveness
   B. Preparing materials and methods
     1. Determining objectives
     2. Determining suitability for intended audience
     3. Developing content and strategies
     4. Assessing the learning environments
     5. Designing the materials and methods
   C. Administering the program
     1. Establishing structures
     2. Selecting training providers
     3. Selecting training facilities
     4. Obtaining financial support
     5. Using consultants

D. Implementing the program activities
1. Introductions
2. Establishing learning objectives
3. Disseminating content
   a. Basic skill-building
      (1) Communicating effectively
         (a) Identification of problems
         (b) Listening skills
         (c) Developing empathy
         (d) Giving and getting information and feedback
         (e) Concentrating on the problem or task
         (f) Developing different perspectives
      (2) Making decisions with the customer
         (a) Goal-setting
         (b) Making plans for action
      (3) Taking action with the customer
         (a) Implementing the action plan
         (b) Providing support
         (c) Making referrals
         (d) Evaluating the results
   b. Ongoing training and confidence-building
      (1) Personal assessment of styles and skills
      (2) Assertiveness training
         (a) Self-esteem and self-responsibility
         (b) Conflict resolution
         (c) Dealing with complaints and criticism
         (d) Practicing assertive behaviors
      (3) Dealing with difficult customer behavior
         (a) Varieties of difficult behavior
         (b) Aggressive behavior
         (c) Passive behavior
         (d) Mental or emotional illness
         (e) Socioeconomic and cultural differences
   c. Stress management
      (1) Self-assessment
      (2) Building support networks
      (3) Coping with stress
      (4) Controlling stress
      (5) Reducing stress
E. Evaluation and Follow-up
1. Trainee evaluation
2. Provider evaluation
3. Transfer of training

Whether libraries approach continuing education and training in interpersonal skills as a whole process, in successive stages, or by focusing on specific topics, there are many excellent resources available to assist managers in the planning. Some of the most highly recommended items are listed in the bibliography at the end of this book.[2]

## CONCLUSION

Awareness and understanding of your own behavioral patterns are valuable first steps towards both changing your own patterns and dealing more effectively with the difficult behavior of others. Either goal requires a willingness to accept the risks and the potential rewards of change. Remember that the Chinese character for crisis contains the symbols for both danger and opportunity.

Once you become aware of the role you play in both successful and difficult interactions with others, you are truly at a turning point, where you must elect either to answer the challenge of change or to maintain status quo. Only the individual can decide if the potential values and rewards are worth the necessary risk-taking and conscious commitment of time and effort.

## References

1. Carl R. Rogers, *Client-Centered Therapy* (Boston: Houghton Mifflin, 1965).
2. Among the most useful for planning interpersonal skills training in a library context are Barbara Conroy, *Library Staff Development and Continuing Education: Principles and Practices* (Littleton, CO: Libraries Unlimited, 1978); Sheila Dainow and Caroline Bailey, *Developing Skills with People: Training for Person to Person Client Contact* (Chichester: John Wiley and Sons, Ltd., 1988); *Guidelines for Quality in Continuing Education for Information, Library and Media Personnel* (Chicago: ALA/Continuing Education Subcommittee of the Standing Committee on Library Education, January 12, 1988); Charles A. Salter and Jeffrey L. Salter, *On the Frontlines: Coping with the Library's Problem Patrons* (Englewood, CO: Libraries Unlimited, 1988); and *Staff Development: A Practical Guide* 2nd ed., Ed. Anne G. Lipow and Deborah A. Carver (Chicago: ALA, 1992).

# APPENDIX A

## TAKING CHARGE OF YOUR OWN BEHAVIOR: A SELF-ASSESSMENT QUIZ

The following self-assessment quiz was *not* designed to be a valid, scientific personality inventory. It is offered here as an informal means of identifying your typical pattern or style of interactive behavior.

(Circle the answer that most closely describes your *immediate*—spontaneous—reaction to each situation.)

1. Two of the people I work with cannot seem to get along with each other. One of them is our boss; the other is a co-worker who does nothing but complain to me about the boss. This is putting me in a bad mood and interfering with my work. I would:
   a. Disregard my co-worker's complaints.
   b. Listen to my co-worker's complaints and help him or her think of ideas for solving his or her problems with the boss and improving their relationship.
   c. Offer my co-worker advice on getting along with the boss.
   d. Try to offer encouragement, cover up my co-worker's deficiencies at work, and go out of my way to be nice to the boss.
2. I am a member of a task force representing all areas and levels of the library. Our task is to draw up new procedures for dealing with disruptive patron behavior. Another member of the task force has just proposed an idea that I think is absurd and impractical. No one else has raised an objection to the idea. I would:
   a. Withhold comment and hope that the absurdity of the idea will eventually become obvious to everyone.
   b. Ask questions about the idea, initiating a discussion in which my reservations about the idea could emerge and be resolved.
   c. Tell the person and the rest of the group just how ridiculous the idea is, and put forth an alternative suggestion.
   d. Say something humorous, making light of the idea, but go along with the group.
3. I am in a group situation in which the discussion has gotten very intense and serious. I would:

   a. Withdraw as unobtrusively as I can.

   b. Participate in the discussion with the same level of intensity and sincerity as the rest of the group.

   c. Attempt to bring the meeting to a swift conclusion.

   d. Change the topic to something lighter, or tell a funny story to elevate the mood of the group.

4. As a supervisor, I notice that one of the most dependable, effective employees in my unit has arrived late for work everyday for the past week. I would:

   a. Ignore the tardiness and hope that whatever problems are causing the tardiness will work themselves out.

   b. Take the employee aside and find out what is going on, remind him or her about the library's personnel policy on tardiness, and with the employee work out a solution to the problem.

   c. Teach the employee (and my other subordinates) a lesson by reprimanding him or her in front of the others.

   d. Cover for the employee with his or her co-workers and with higher management, before I find out why he or she is late.

5. When I come into the library staff room in the morning, I like a fresh cup of coffee. Although I am usually early for work, other people often arrive even earlier and empty the pot before I have a chance to get there. They sometimes fail to brew another pot, and I end up having to make it for myself. I would:

   a. Say nothing to the other coffee drinkers, but fume internally, and resolve to come to work as early as I can.

   b. Talk over the problem with the other coffee drinkers and agree upon a plan to solve the empty-pot problem.

   c. Find out who drank the last cup without making another pot and confront him or her about it on the spot.

   d. Make jokes about an empty-pot syndrome to the others, but continue to brew my own coffee without discussing the problem as such.

6. I am working with others on a problem when I discover that some important and readily available information needed by the group is missing. Getting that information was not my responsibility; someone else has neglected to obtain it. The lack of information has put a strain on the group's efforts. I would:

    a. Say and do nothing but secretly relish the group's collective annoyance.

    b. Verbally acknowledge the significance of the missing information and offer to get it immediately.

    c. Demand that the person who failed to obtain the needed information confess and make sure he or she knows how this irresponsibility has set back the group's efforts.

    d. Make light of the situation to relieve some of the group's worry, noting that "these things happen" but that "things usually work out OK in the end."

7. I have been having some personal problems in the past few weeks and, as a result, have been feeling somewhat depressed and tired. On a number of occasions, some of my co-workers have had to take up the slack for me on the job. They have been asking me questions and trying to find out what the problem is. I would:

    a. Tell them that it's personal and that I will work things out for myself.

    b. Tell them what is going on with me and ask for their patience and help in getting back in the groove at work.

    c. Tell them that I'll be better soon, and that they should mind their own business and leave me alone.

    d. Make light of my personal situation, apologize for inconveniencing them, and vow to carry my share of the workload.

8. My boss just hired a person who is several years younger than I am, someone who shows considerable promise for leadership as well as skill in doing the work. There is a good chance that the boss is grooming this person to take over my department soon. I would:

    a. Resent the boss's doing this to me and consider finding another job.

    b. Find out what it takes to get a promotion and work toward it or toward another higher position in the organization.

    c. Do what I could to slow down this person's progress.

    d. Get as close to the person as possible, making us friends.

9. My boss has asked me to develop a revised policy and procedure for patron services. The job is quite complicated and takes a great deal of attention to detail and skill, but I finish ahead of schedule. It is adopted throughout

the library system, and I receive recognition and reward for my accomplishment. I would:

   a. Keep quietly to myself and try to avoid a lot of attention.

   b. Feel pleased with myself and accept whatever recognition I receive.

   c. Let everyone know how difficult the assignment was, and that I deserve a lot more recognition than I've received.

   d. Make light of my accomplishment.

10. My supervisor is poking fun at me and embarrassing me in the presence of other members of our department because I made a couple of critical mistakes yesterday. The situation is making me very uncomfortable. I would:

   a. Say nothing, but inwardly wish the supervisor a rotten day.

   b. Admit yesterday's mistakes and, when the others have moved on, ask my supervisor to meet with me privately to talk about my feelings.

   c. Get upset and angry and threaten to leave unless the supervisor stops.

   d. Make light of it and laugh along with everyone else.

## QUIZ ANALYSIS

Add the number of a's, b's, c's and d's you have circled. The letter circled most frequently symbolizes your primary interactive behavioral style, as described in Chapter 2 of this book.

The more *b*'s you circled, the closer your behavior resembles *effective* Type I behavior, the more likely you are to feel in control of your behavior when you interact with others, and the less likely you are to experience other people as difficult. If your highest score was in the *b* (Type IV), *c* (Type II), or *d* (Type III) categories, it is quite possible that you are generating at least *some* of the difficulty you are experiencing with other people.

**Source:** This quiz was inspired by a similar quiz developed by Donald H. Weiss for inclusion in his handbook, *How To Deal With Difficult People* (New York: American Management Association, 1987).

# APPENDIX B

## RECOMMENDED READING ON SELECTED NON-TRADITIONAL LIBRARY USER GROUPS

### THE HOMELESS POOR

Barr, Peter B., et al. "Perceptual Attitudes of a Charitable Organization: An Investigative Approach," *Health Marketing Quarterly*, Vol. 8, 1991, pp. 81-95.

Behrmann, Christine, et al. "The Library Serves Homeless Children," *The Bookmark*, Vol. 46, Spring 1988, pp. 198-199.

Biasi, Gary L. "Social Policy and Social Science Research on Homelessness," *Journal of Social Issues*, Vol. 46, 1990, pp. 207-219.

Bidinotto, Robert J. "Don't Be Mislead by the Prevalent Myths About the Homeless," *Reader's Digest*, Vol. 138, June 1991, pp. 98-103.

Breakey, William R., et al. "Health and Mental Health Problems of Homeless Men and Women in Baltimore," *Journal of the American Medical Association*, Vol. 262, September 8, 1989, pp. 1352-1357.

Burt, Martha A., and Barbara E. Cohen, "Differences Among Homeless Single Women, Women with Children, and Single Men," *Social Problems*, Vol. 36, December 1989, pp. 508-549.

Dexheimer, Lynda. "Look Who's Helping the Homeless," *Association Management*, Vol. 40, December 1988, pp. 28-38.

Chatman, Elfreda A. "Opinion Leadership, Poverty, and Information Sharing," *RQ*, Vol. 26, Spring 1987, pp. 341-353.

Ferguson, Sarah. "Us vs. Them: America's Growing Frustration with the Homeless," *Utne Reader*, September 1990, pp. 50-55.

Fitzpatrick, Jean G. "Mommy, Are Homeless People Bad?" *Parents*, Vol. 64, February 1989, pp. 94-100.

Gibson, Richard S. "Broken Brothers and Breaking Stereotypes: How Can We Respond to Homeless People as They Are Instead of as They 'Ought' to Be?" *Public Welfare*, Vol. 49, Spring 1991, pp. 34-41.

Gore, Albert, Jr. "Public Policy and the Homeless," *American Psychologist*, Vol. 34, August 1990, pp. 960-962.

Greiner, Joy M. "The Homeless: PLA Members' Consensus is for Equitable Services and Respect," *Public Libraries*, Vol. 28, May/June 1989, pp. 137-141.

Hilfiker, David. "Commentary/Caring for the Poor: Are We Comfortable With Homelessness?" *Journal of the American Medical Association*, Vol. 262, September 8, 1989, pp. 1375-1376.

Jacoby, Tamar. "Thinking About the Homeless," *Dissent*, Vol. 38, Spring 1991, pp. 249-253.

Janes, Phoebe, and Ellen Meltzer. "Origins and Attitudes: Training Reference Librarians for a Pluralistic World," *Reference Librarian*, Vol. 30, 1990, pp. 145-155.

Kuehn, Jennifer J. "Homelessness: Interdisciplinary Collection Development Challenge," *Collection Building*, Vol. 11, No. 1, n.d., pp. 14-18.

Landers, Robert K. "Why Homeless Need More Than Shelter," *Editorial Research Reports*, March 30, 1990, pp. 174-184.

Lee, Barrett A., et al. "Public Beliefs About the Causes of Homelessness," *Social Forces*, Vol. 69, September 1990, pp. 253-265.

Nassimbeni, Mary. "Libraries and Poverty," *South African Journal of Library and Information Science*, Vol. 54, June 1986, pp. 56-60.

"Overview: A Challenge to our Conscience," *Scholastic Update* (Teacher's Edition), Vol. 121, February 10, 1989, p. 2.

Owens, Major. "The War on Poverty and Community Outreach," *Activism in American Librarianship*, 1962-1973. (Westport, CT: Greenwood Press, 1987).

Potter, Bruce. "East Orange Foregoes Traditional Models," *Public Welfare*, Vol. 47, Winter 1989, pp. 13-15.

Rochman, Hazel. "Connections: Poor, Pure, and Iinvisible," *Booklist* Vol. 87, April 1, 1991, p. 1567.

Rossi, Peter H. *Down and Out in America: The Origins of Homelessness.* (Chicago: University of Chicago Press, 1989).

_____. "The Old Homeless and the New Homelessness in Historical Perspective," *American Psychologist*, Vol. 45, August 1990, pp. 954-959.

_____, and James D. Wright. "The Determinants of Homelessness," *Health Affairs*, Vol. 6, Spring 1987, pp. 19-32.

Sapp, Gregg. "Some Editorial Thoughts . . . on Sleeping in the Library," *Idaho Librarian*, Vol. 41, July 1989, p. 54.

Simmons, Randall C. "The Homeless in the Public Library: Implications for Access to Libraries," *RQ*, Vol. 25, Fall 1985, pp. 110-120.

Sosin, Michael R. "Homelessness in Chicago: A Study Sheds New Light on an Old Problem," *Public Welfare*, Vol. 47, Winter 1989, pp. 22-28.

Stagner, M., and H. Richman. *General Assistance Families* (Chicago: National Opinion Research Center, 1985).

Torrey, E. Fuller. *Nowhere To Go: The Tragic Odyssey of the Homeless Mentally Ill.* (New York: Harper and Row, 1988).

White, Herbert S. "'Send These, the Homeless, Tempest-Tost to Me,'" *Library Journal*, Vol. 114, February 15, 1989, pp. 146-147.

## THE "LATCHKEY" CHILD

Anderson, A. J. "Suffer the Children (The Library Is Not a Free Alternative to Day Care Centers)," *Library Journal*, Vol. 113, November 15, 1988, pp. 47-48.

Callaghan, Linda W. "Children's Services—What Do They Mean to the Rest of the Profession," *American Libraries*, Vol. 19, February 1988, pp. 102-103.

Chepesiuk, Ronald J. "Reaching Out: The Greenville County Library's Latchkey Kids Program," *Library Journal*, Vol. 112, March 1, 1987, pp. 46-48.

Dowd, Frances Smardo. *Latchkey Children in the Library and Community: Issues, Strategies, and Programs.* (Phoenix, AZ: Oryx Press, 1991).

Fuqua, Christopher S. "Unattended Children: An Engagement Policy That Works," *Wilson Library Bulletin*, Vol. 62, June 1988, pp. 88-90.

Goldberg, Beverly. "Survey of Large PLs Helps Define Latchkey Challenge," *American Libraries*, Vol. 19, November 1988, p. 836.

Mueller, William. "Kid Stuff: A Policy That Works for Two Cities," *Library Journal*, Vol. 112, March 1, 1987, pp. 48-51.

Noble, Kenneth B. "Library as Daycare: New Curbs and Concerns," *New York Times*, 15 February 1988, A1+.

Public Library Association/Service to Children Committee. *Latchkey Children in the Public Library: Resources for Planners.* (Chicago: American Library Association, 1989).

U. S. Bureau of the Census. *After-School Care of School-Age Children: December, 1984.* Series P-23, No. 149. (Washington, DC: U. S. Government Printing Office, 1985).

Weingand, Darlene E. *The Organic Public Library.* (Littleton, CO: Libraries Unlimited, 1984).

# APPENDIX C

## GUIDELINES FOR THE DEVELOPMENT OF POLICIES AND PROCEDURES REGARDING USER BEHAVIOR AND LIBRARY USAGE

American Library Associaiton, January 24, 1993

### Introduction

Libraries are faced with problems of user behavior that must be addressed to insure the effective delivery of service and full access to facilities. Library governing bodies must approach the regulation of user behavior within the framework of the ALA Code of Professional Ethics, the Library Bill of Rights and the law, including local and state statutes, constitutional standards under the First and Fourteenth Amendments, due process and equal treatment under the law.

Publicly supported library service is based upon the First Amendment right of free expression. Publicly supported libraries are recognized as limited public forums for access to information. At least one federal court of appeals has recognized a First Amendment right to receive information in a public library. Library policies and procedures that could impinge upon such rights are subject to a higher standard of review than may be required in the policies of other public services and facilities.

There is a significant government interest in maintaining a library environment that is conducive to all users' exercise of their constitutionally protected right to receive information. This significant interest authorizes publicly supported libraries to maintain a safe and healthy environment in which library users and staff can be free from harassment, intimidation, and threats to their safety and well-being. Libraries should provide appropriate safeguards against such behavior and enforce policies and procedures addressing that behavior when it occurs.

In order to protect all library users' right of access to library facilities, to ensure the safety of users and staff, and to protect library resources and facilities from damage, the library's governing authority may impose reasonable restrictions on the time, place, or manner of library access.

### Guidelines

The American Library Association's Intellectual Freedom Committee recommends that publicly supported libraries use the following guidelines, based upon constitutional principles, to develop policies and procedures governing the use of library facilities:

1. Libraries are advised to rely upon existing legislation and law enforcement mechanisms as the primary means of controlling behavior that involves public safety, criminal behavior, or other issues covered by existing local, state, or federal statutes. In many instances, this legal framework may be sufficient to provide the library with the necessary tools to maintain order.

2. If the library's governing body chooses to write its own policies and procedures regarding user behavior or access to library facilities, services, and resources, the policies should cite statutes or ordinances upon which the authority to make those policies is based.

3. Library policies and procedures governing the use of library facilities should be carefully examined to insure that they are not in violation of the LIBRARY BILL OF RIGHTS.

4. Reasonable and narrowly drawn policies and procedures designed to prohibit interference with use of the facilities and services by others, or to prohibit activities inconsistent with achievement of substantial library objectives, are acceptable.

5. Such policies and the attendant implementing procedures should be reviewed regularly by the library's legal counsel for compliance with federal and state constitutional requirements, federal and state civil rights legislation, all other applicable federal and state legislation, and applicable case law.

6. Every effort should be made to respond to potentially difficult circumstances of user behavior in a timely, direct, and open manner. Common sense, reason, and sensitivity should be used to resolve issues in a constructive and positive manner without escalation.

7. Libraries should develop an ongoing staff training program based upon their user behavior policy. This program should include training to develop empathy and understanding of the social and economic problems of some library users.

8. Policies and regulations that impose restrictions on library access:
   a. should apply only to those activities that materially interfere with the public's right of access to library facilities, the safety of users and staff, and the protection of library resources and facilities;

b. should narrowly tailor prohibitions or restrictions so that they are not more restrictive than needed to serve their objectives;

c. should attempt to balance competing interests and avoid favoring the majority at the expense of individual rights, or allowing individual users' rights to supersede those of the majority of library users;

d. should be based upon actual behavior and not upon arbitrary distinctions between individuals or classes of individuals. Policies should not target specific users or groups of users based upon an assumption or expectation that such users might engage in behaviors that could disrupt library service;

e. should not restrict access to the library by persons who merely inspire the anger or annoyance of others. Policies based upon appearance or behavior that is merely annoying, or which merely generates negative subjective reactions from others, do not meet the necessary standard unless the behavior would interfere with access by an objectively reasonable person to library facilities and services. Such policies should employ a reasonable, objective standard based on the behavior itself;

f. must provide a clear description of the behavior that is prohibited so that a reasonably intelligent person will have fair warning and must be continuously and clearly communicated in an effective manner to all library users;

g. to the extent possible, should not leave those affected without adequate alternative means of access to information in the library;

h. must be enforced evenhandedly, and not in a manner intended to benefit or disfavor any person or group in an arbitrary or capricious manner.

The user behaviors addressed in these guidelines are the result of a wide variety of individual and societal conditions. Libraries should take advantage of the expertise of local social service agencies, advocacy groups, mental health professionals, law enforcement officials, and other community resources to develop community strategies for addressing the needs of a diverse population.

*Reprinted by permission of the American Library Association*

# BIBLIOGRAPHY AND TRAINING RESOURCE LIST

## MONOGRAPHS

Bach, George R. and Herb Goldberg. *Creative Aggression.* Garden City, NY: Doubleday, 1974.

Benjamin, Alfred. *The Helping Interview.* 3rd Edition. Boston: Houghton Mifflin Company, 1981.

Berne, Eric. *Games People Play.* New York: Grove Press, 1964.

———. *What Do You Say After You Say Hello?.* New York: Grove Press, 1972.

Bisno, Herb. *Managing Conflict.* (Sage Human Services Guide, 52) Newbury Park, CA: Sage Publications, 1988.

Blake, Robert R., and Jane Srygley Mouton. *Solving Costly Organizational Conflicts.* San Francisco: Jossey-Bass Publishers, 1984.

Bramson, Robert M. *Coping with Difficult People.* New York: Ballantine Books, 1981.

Burton, John W. *Resolving Deep-Rooted Conflict: A Handbook.* Lanham, MD: University Press of America, 1987.

*Conflict and Cooperation in Management.* Boston: Harvard Business Press, Reprint Department #12021, 1973.

*Conflict Management and Problem Solving: Interpersonal to International Applications.* Edited by Dennis J. D. Sandole and Ingrid Sandole-Staroste. New York: New York University Press, 1987.

Conroy, Barbara. *Library Staff Development and Continuing Education: Principles and Practices.* Littleton, CO: Libraries Unlimited, 1978.

———, and Barbara Schindler Jones. *Improving Communication in the Library.* Phoenix, AZ: Oryx Press, 1986.

Coombs, Clyde H., and George S. Avrunin. *The Structure of Conflict.* Hillsdale, NJ: Lawrence Erlbaum Associates, Publishers, 1988.

Covey, Stephen R. *The Seven Habits of Highly Effective People: Restoring the Character Ethic.* New York: Simon and Schuster, 1990.

Daniels, Tom D., and Barry K. Spiker. *Perspectives on Organizational Communication.* Dubuque, IA: Wm. C. Brown Publishers, 1987.

Dainow, Sheila, and Caroline Bailey. *Developing Skills with People: Training for Person to Person Client Contact.* Chichester: John Wiley and Sons, Ltd., 1988.

DeHart, Florence E. *The Librarian's Psychological Commitments: Human Relations in Librarianship.* (Contributions in Librarianship and Information Science, Number 27) Westport, CT: Greenwood Press, 1979.

DeVito, Joseph A. *The Interpersonal Communication Book.* 6th Edition. New York: HarperCollins, 1992.

*Discover the World: Empowering Children to Value Themselves, Others and the Earth.* Edited by Susan Hopkins and Jeffry Winters. Philadelphia: New Society Publishers, 1990.

Dowd, Frances Smardo. *Latchkey Children in the Library and Community: Issues, Strategies, and Programs.* Phoenix, AZ: Oryx Press, 1991.

Fraser, Niall M., and Keith W. Hipel. *Conflict Analysis: Models and Resolutions.* (North Holland Series in System Science and Engineering, Volume 11) New York: North Holland, 1984.

*Guidelines for Quality in Continuing Education for Information, Library and Media Personnel.* Chicago: American Library Association/Continuing Education Subcommittee of the Standing Committee on Library Education, January 12, 1988.

Jandt, Fred Edmund. *Win-Win Negotiating: Turning Conflict into Agreement.* With the assistance of Paul Gillette. New York: John Wiley and Sons, 1985.

Johnson, David W. *Reaching Out: Interpersonal Effectiveness and Self Actualization.* 3rd Edition. Englewood Cliffs, NJ: Prentice-Hall, 1986.

Keating, Charles J. *Dealing With Difficult People: How You Can Come Out on Top in Personality Conflicts.* New York: Paulist Press, 1984.

*Library Communication: The Language of Leadership.* Ed. Donald E. Riggs. Chicago: American Library Association, 1991.

Lustberg, Arch. *Winning at Confrontation*. Washington, DC: Association Department, U. S. Chamber of Commerce, 1985.

Mathews, Anne J. *Communicate! A Librarian's Guide to Interpersonal Relations*. Chicago: American Library Association, 1983.

Moore, Christopher W. *The Mediation Process: Practical Strategies for Resolving Conflict*. San Francisco: Jossey-Bass Publishers, 1986.

Munter, Mary. *Guide to Managerial Communication*. 2nd Edition. Englewood Cliffs, NJ: Prentice-Hall, Inc., 1987.

Piaget, Gerald W. *Control Freaks: Who They Are and How to Stop Them from Running Your Life*. New York: Doubleday, 1991.

Powell, Judith W., and Robert B. LeLieuvre. *Peoplework: Communications Dynamics for Librarians*. Chicago: American Library Association, 1979.

*Public Relations for Libraries: Essays in Communications Techniques*. (Contributions in Librarianship and Information Science, Number 5) Westport, CT: Greenwood Press, 1973.

Rahim, M. Afzalur. *Managing Conflict in Organizations*. New York: Praeger, 1986.

*Reader in Library Communication*. Ed. Mary B. Cassata and Roger Cain Palmer. Englewood, CO: Information Handling Services, Library and Education Division, 1976.

Rossi, Peter H. *Down and Out in America: the Origins of Homelessness*. Chicago: University of Chicago Press, 1989.

Salter, Charles A. and Jeffrey L. Salter. *On the Frontlines: Coping with the Library's Problem Patron*. Englewood, CO: Libraries Unlimited, 1988.

Sanford, John A. *Between People: Communicating One-to-One*. New York: Paulist Press, 1982.

Shuman, Bruce A. *Riverbend Revisited: The Problem Patron in the Library*. Phoenix, AZ: Oryx Press, 1984.

Solomon, Muriel. *Working with Difficult People*. Englewood Cliffs, NJ: Prentice-Hall, 1990.

*Staff Development: A Practical Guide*. 2nd Edition. Ed. Anne G. Lipow and Deborah A. Carver. Chicago: American Library Association, 1992.

Tavris, Carol. *Anger: the Misunderstood Emotion*. Rev. Edition. New York: Simon and Schuster, 1989.

*Theory and Research in Conflict Management*. Ed. M. Afzalur Rahim. New York: Praeger, 1990.

Tjosvold, Dean. *The Conflict-Positive Organization: Stimulate Diversity and Create Unity*. Reading, MA: Addison-Wesley Publishing Company, 1991.

Torrey, E. Fuller. *Nowhere to Go: the Tragic Odyssey of the Homeless Mentally Ill*. New York: Harper and Row, 1988.

Ury, William L., Jeanne M. Brett, and Stephen B. Goldberg. *Getting Disputes Resolved: Designing Systems to Cut the Costs of Conflict*. San Francisco: Jossey-Bass Publishers, 1989.

Walton, Richard E. *Managing Conflict: Interpersonal Dialogue and Third-Party Roles*. Reading, MA: Addison-Wesley Publishing Company, 1987.

Weiss, Donald H. *How to Deal with Difficult People*. New York: American Management Association, 1987.

Yates, Douglas, Jr. *The Politics of Management*. San Francisco: Jossey-Bass Publishers, 1985.

Zaleznik, Abraham. *The Managerial Mystique: Restoring Leadership in Business*. New York: Harper and Row, 1989.

# VIDEORECORDINGS

Brinkman, Rick, and Rick Kirschner. *How to Deal with Difficult People*. Volume I: *Strategies and Tactics for Dealing with Difficult People* (74 minutes). Volume II: *Dealing with the Ten Most Difficult People* (116 minutes). Boulder, CO: Career Track, 1988. Videocassettes, VHS

*Difficult People: How to Deal with Them* (38 minutes). West Des Moines, IA: White Leopard Video, 1989. Videocassette, VHS

*The Library Survival Guide: Managing the Problem Situation* (20 minutes). Chicago: American Library Association/Library Video Network, 1987. Videocassette, VHS

*Nice Guys Finish First* (50 minutes). Chicago: Films Incorporated, 1986. Videocassette, VHS

---

# SOUNDRECORDINGS

Bramson, Robert M. *Coping with Difficult People.* (Six audiocassettes) New York: Simon and Schuster Audio Publishing, 1986.

Covey, Stephen R. *The 7 Habits of Highly Effective People.* (Six audiocassettes) Provo, UT: Covey Leadership Center, 1990.

Tavris, Carol. *Controlling Anger: How to Turn Anger Into Positive Action.* (Four audiocassettes) Boulder, CO: CareerTrack, Inc., 1989.

# INDEX